# LOOMS AND TEXTILES OF THE COPTS

First Millennium
Egyptian Textiles in the
Carl Austin Rietz Collection
of the California
Academy of Sciences

Diane Lee Carroll

Memoir Number 11
Published by the California Academy of Sciences
Distributed by the University of Washington Press, Seattle and London

BOOK DESIGN
AND PRODUCTION:
Dustin Kahn

PHOTOGRAPHY:
Susan Middleton

CALLIGRAPHY:
John Prestianni

ILLUSTRATION:
Amy Pertschuk
Diane Carroll

COPY EDITING:
Katherine Ulrich
Ruth Weine

PROOFREADING:
Mary Christine Cunningham

SCIENTIFIC
PUBLICATIONS
COMMITTEE:
Daphne Fautin, *Scientific Editor*
Frank Almeda
Luis Baptista
Wojciech Pulawski
Frank Talbot, *Executive Director,*
    California Academy of Sciences
Sheridan Warrick

Date submitted for publication: July 8, 1986
Date accepted for publication: September 24, 1986

Published by the California Academy of Sciences.
This project was supported by two grants from the
National Endowment for the Arts (22-4420-076 and 32-4420-00126)
and by the Carl Austin Rietz Food Technology Foundation.

ISBN 0-295-96672-6
Library of Congress Catalog Card Number 88-070639

COVER: *Fragment of a Tapestry Square
from a Cushion (Rietz Number 28)*

fco

# C O N T E N T S

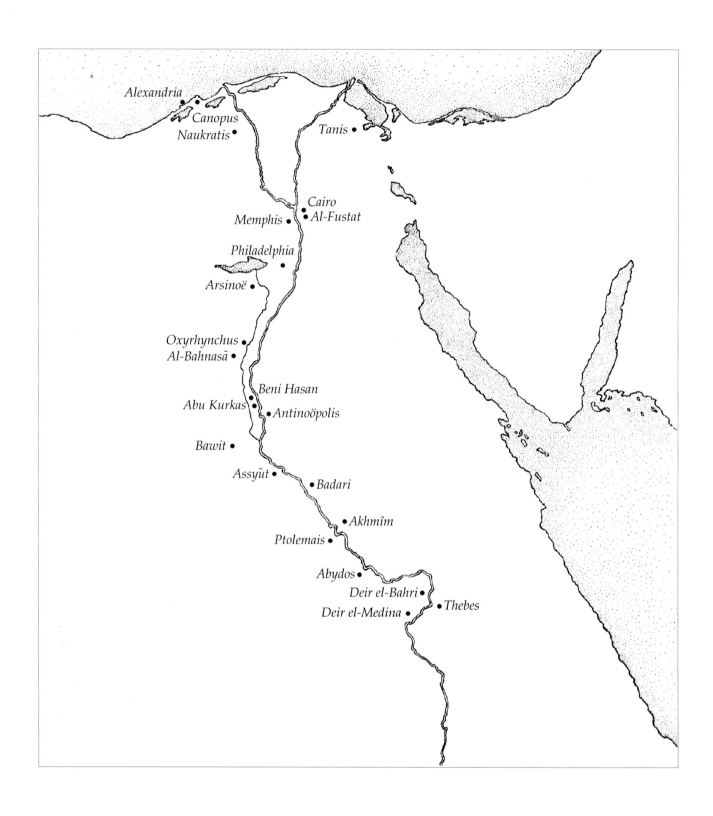

Alexandria

Canopus

Naukratis

Tanis

Cairo
Al-Fustat

Memphis

Philadelphia

Arsinoë

Oxyrhynchus

Al-Bahnasā

Beni Hasan

Abu Kurkas

Antinoöpolis

Bawit

Assyūt

Badari

Akhmîm

Ptolemais

Abydos

Deir el-Bahri

Deir el-Medina

Thebes

# INTRODUCTION

T HE WEAVER'S ART is an ancient one, its history rooted in the remote past. Tracing the path of this history from its distant beginnings is a difficult undertaking, largely because textile materials are highly perishable. There are long gaps in the record. The conditions that prevail at most archaeological sites do not favor the preservation of textiles in their original form. Rare indeed are the special situations needed to protect textiles from complete destruction: dry caves, watertight tombs, or a region without significant rainfall. Because of textile preservation problems, some phases of the history of weaving must be recovered almost entirely by means of secondary sources, principally depictions in art, and tools—bobbins, needles, spindle whorls, bone awls, and the like. Even here there are problems because many weaving tools were made of perishable materials as well.

Egyptian textile technology is better documented than most. The climate, geography, and burial customs of Egypt have favored the preservation of textiles. Fragments have been found that could have been woven as early as the fourth millennium B.C. (Brunton and Caton-Thompson 1928). Many have been found in dynastic burials, either as mummy wrappings or as grave goods. Though not every period is represented equally well, the surviving textiles are sufficiently plentiful to offer historians a nearly unique opportunity to study a large group of technically related

textiles, woven at different dates, which can be understood to form a more or less connected series. Among the most recent of the surviving specimens of cloth in this series are those labeled "Coptic." Most of these are thought to derive from burials that, luckily, had been placed well above local water tables and far enough away from the Nile to have remained unaffected by this river's annual flooding. At least 20,000 textiles—a few whole, the majority fragmentary—are estimated to exist in public and private collections (Lewis 1969:7). Some authorities claim the number of extant Coptic textiles to be even greater, closer to 100,000 (Gervers 1977). Examples can be found in virtually every major collection of textiles as well as in many lesser ones (Lubell 1976–1977).

The particular specimens belonging to the Coptic textile corpus that are the focus of attention here were collected by Carl Austin Rietz, presumably purchased during a trip to Egypt in the late 1920s. Details concerning their acquisition are unknown. All specimens are fragments, representing a total of 72 textiles. Optical microscope examination of fibers from the textiles revealed that 25 of the textiles are wool with wool ornamentation, 46 of them are linen with wool or wool and linen ornamentation, and 1 is silk. They range in date from approximately the late third or early fourth century to the eleventh or twelfth century. By early medieval times, Coptic weavers yet remaining in Egypt were well into the process of adapting their designs and technology to conform to Egyptian Islamic tastes (Golombek and Gervers 1977), and the distinctive characteristics of Coptic textiles gradually vanished. Coptic textiles believed to be older than the earliest Rietz specimens exist, but they are rare.

Because of the size of the Coptic textile corpus and the long time span involved, some researchers divide it into three or more groups according to the age of the individual textiles. In one system, the textiles assigned to the earlier group are termed "Greco-Roman." Because they sometimes depict Christian motifs, the term Coptic is reserved for textiles believed to have been woven later (Trilling 1982). Other systems divide the corpus to correspond with contemporary art styles, specifically, late Antique, late Roman, and early Byzantine, this last corresponding to Coptic (Kendrick 1920, 1921, 1922). While logical, these systems have the disadvantage of being overprecise, considering the present state of knowledge about the textiles. It is difficult to date most of them with any exactness, even specimens known to derive from an archaeological context. At present there is almost no unanimity in dating all the different varieties of Egyptian textiles woven during the centuries in question. Dating systems based upon style present particular problems: Some late classical design elements remained popular for centuries (Grube 1962). Until the dating problem is closer to being solved, it appears best to retain the term Coptic for all the textiles.

Another point, the indigenous people who lived in Egypt during the first millennium have been, by long-established custom, termed Copts, to distinguish them from the Egyptians of the pre-Christian era. Interestingly, the word Copt itself is of disputed origin. One convincing argument claims that both Egypt and Copt derive from the Greek word for Egypt, *aigyptos*, eventually shortened to *gypt*. The original definition of Copt, then, was simply Egyptian, but by the time of the Arab conquest in the seventh century over 90 percent of the Egyptian population was Christian, and so Copt came to have the meaning of Christian, rather than Egyptian. In the early centuries of the Christian Era this interpretation had not yet evolved, and the majority of Copts were not Christians. For this study of Egyptian textiles of the early Christian Era, the ancient meaning of the word has been retained, and Copt is used to identify established residents of Egypt who lived after the birth of Christ, whether of pure Egyptian descent or pure or mixed Macedonian-Greek or Roman descent. Coptic textiles, by this definition, are primarily the products of people who lived in Egypt during the early centuries of the Christian Era but who were not necessarily Christian in their personal beliefs.

THE VARIETY and often colorful appearance of Coptic textiles have made them attractive to collectors. The majority of these textiles are embellished with motifs worked in dyed yarn. These motifs are of a number of types, often distinctly different in appearance though the techniques used to produce them may be similar. In some, the main designs consist of human or animal figures, crudely outlined but frequently exhibiting an engaging naïveté. There are several such examples in the Rietz Collection, among them, Numbers 27, 33, and 40. Other designs are formal in appearance, with floral motifs and geometric figures precisely rendered. Notable Rietz specimens are Numbers 4, 6, 10, and 18. There are numerous variants.

Specimens of Coptic textiles in different states of preservation, whole, partially preserved, and in fragments, have been actively collected since the late eighteenth century. Examples in some major European museums were recovered by the archaeologists who accompanied Napoleon during his campaign in Egypt in 1798–1799. During the nineteenth and twentieth centuries, Coptic textiles were acquired by numerous museums. Some museums located in textile-manufacturing centers—for example, Lyons in France, Halifax in England, and more recently, Tokyo in Japan—made a point of amassing textile collections for study and now house particularly handsome specimens of Coptic textiles. During the same period many private collections were formed, including the Rietz Collection now in the California Academy of Sciences.

Although Coptic textiles are representatives of a class of ancient artifacts rarely found in other parts of the Near East and the shores of the Mediterranean, they have received comparatively little serious attention. Exhibits of Coptic textiles tend to emphasize their decorative rather than their historical aspects. The majority of the longer publications devoted to Coptic textiles have been collection or exhibition catalogs intended primarily to record appearances and construction details, seldom attempting to suggest how contemporary happenings may have shaped the lives and thinking of the people who designed and once owned them.

Many historians do not see textiles as having significance, either to history in general or to the history of art in particular. In works devoted to specific periods of art history, textiles, if discussed at all, are treated as a minor art form lacking the status of architecture, sculpture, or painting. Coptic art itself may be looked upon as a provincial version of late Roman art, a viewpoint not dispelled by the remains of Coptic buildings and sculpture that yet survive. While the prevailing style of these is likely to convey a feeling of strength and vigor, with design elements organized in ways that may be pleasing to the eye, the overall effect is frequently unsophisticated, even clumsy, especially when compared with fine examples of the Hellenized art of the early Roman Empire such as the *Ara Pacis*. Moreover, the surviving examples of Coptic architecture and sculpture are dwarfed by the serious, formal, and generally massive remains of dynastic Egyptian architecture and sculpture. It is no surprise then, to discover that when it comes to the textiles, even specialists in the field of Coptic art normally limit themselves to mentioning and illustrating only a few of the more colorful and impressive examples, stressing their probable connection with the textiles of Classical antiquity (Wessel 1965; Badawy 1978).

Contributing to this neglect could be the circumstance that comparative material from sites outside Egypt is scant. It consists of fragments such as those found in a chest under the altar of the Cappella Sanctorum in Rome (Kendrick 1920:3) and the earlier textiles found at Dura-Europos in Syria (Pfister and Bellinger 1945) and Palmyra (Pfister 1934–1940). Another cause for neglect could be the fact that few of the many known Coptic textiles derive from formally conducted excavations in which records of the finds were made and published.

The majority of the textiles now in collections come from burials and ancient trash dumps ransacked by unlicensed excavators. These entrepreneurs are prone to separate their discoveries from associated finds, both from other textiles and from artifacts like coins, that might help date particular burials. Dealers in antiquities, and some collectors too, may trim edges or discard plain or damaged areas of incomplete specimens so all that remains of a Coptic garment or domestic textile is a neatly scissored square or rectangle of plain weave with, in the center, a portion of its ornamentation. From such specimens it is rarely possible to identify the original form and purpose of the textile with any degree of confidence. Too often the mutilation has gone even further. In the case of Rietz Numbers 3, 4, 6, 7, and 26, to mention but a handful of the thousands of examples that exist, the plain parts of the textiles have been cut away to the point where specific features of the weave used for the main parts of the textiles can seldom be recovered. Even less helpful, would-be restorers, bringing a paste-pot into play, may combine bits and pieces to make a piece that appears whole at first glance. Number 38 is an example: it is a paste-up made from two, possibly three, unrelated textiles. Less reprehensible is the "restoration" of Number 30. All of its parts derive from the same textile, and the original design was not changed.

Along with the aforesaid activities, dealers may misrepresent the origin of their wares. One understands they do this to protect themselves, their suppliers, and good sources of material, but it seriously compounds the problem of privately excavated textiles. Lacking the pertinent documentation provided by scientific excavation, the prospects for learning anything of value from the remains of Coptic textiles appear discouraging, though not entirely hopeless.

The paucity of attention given to Coptic textiles, for whatever reason, is unfortunately, neglect that would be a loss to knowledge if allowed to continue. Even a brief contemplation of the more obvious features of the textiles is sufficient to arouse curiosity and generate questions. The textiles give every indication of being more than colorful or amusing souvenirs of an important but poorly understood period of history. Why, it might be asked, are there so many different motifs, so many different styles? Did the motifs have meaning to the original users of the textiles, or were they only decoration? Were some of the motifs trademarks or quality symbols? Were all of the textiles labeled Coptic made in Egypt? If they were, how did they compare with contemporary textiles from other countries, in technique, in quality? These and many other questions might be asked, and attempts might be made to find answers. Ancient decorated textiles could, it seems, be information sources for a better understanding of the beliefs and customs of the peoples who once used them. The large corpus of Coptic textiles offers a valuable opportunity for scholars to obtain information unlike that obtainable from the customary sources, the accounts of ancient historians and other ancient writers. Coptic textiles should merit attention for this reason if for no other.

D URING THE FIRST millennium of the present era, when Coptic textiles were being produced, there occurred several of history's more consequential turning points—events that eventually led to major shifts in social attitudes, philosophical systems, and technical processes. As a body, the textiles form a relatively homogeneous record that could, plausibly, supplement the fragmentary, disconnected, and sometimes biased records provided by contemporary written and pictorial material. The information provided by the textiles comes from their materials, technology, and decorative motifs, matters not likely to be subject to later historical revision. In turn, if the textile-derived information can be fitted into the overall historical and social background of the times in which they were made, the textiles themselves might be dated more precisely.

Complementing the surviving textiles are three sources that have received scant attention so far as their connection with Coptic textiles is concerned. The first source is the large and diverse body of nonliterary papyri, some of it contemporary with the textiles, some of it earlier. Quantities of written documents concerning various aspects of daily life in Egypt have survived, preserved, in great part, by the same favorable circumstances that helped to preserve so many textiles, though often, like the textiles, in fragments. Useful introductions to papyrology, covering the distribution and problems of interpretation of the documents, along with possible historical applications and their limitations, appear in Bell (1948) and Turner (1968).

So important was this ancestral form of paper in daily life that, possibly as a result, the papyrus plant, *Cyperus papyrus*, became extinct in the Egyptian wild shortly before A.D. 1000. Changes in climate may have contributed, too. Whatever the cause, either the value of papyrus or its gradually increasing scarcity, short notices and memos were commonly written on substitutes for papyrus—spalls of limestone or pieces of broken pottery, termed *ostraka*. Studies of nonliterary papyri generally include ostraka because the same people, bureaucrats for the greater part wrote on both papyrus and ostraka. Much of what can be learned about the economic and legal aspects of the production of textiles in Egypt during this period is derived from ostraka. Quantities of ostraka have been discovered that record taxes paid by weavers (Samuel 1971:101, 102; Bagnall and Samuel 1976:35-37, 102, 212). The pertinent papyri, which mention weaving and textiles, are primarily legal documents such as apprentice and wedding contracts, divorce settlements, wills, tax records, and permits for weavers. The literature covering the subject is large, often difficult of access, and new documents are added every year. The range of subjects covered by the business papyri has been admirably illustrated by the select collection of papyri published by Hunt and Edgar (1932, 1934). Specific examples will be cited later. In general, the papyri and ostraka demonstrate how all-pervasive textiles were in Egyptian life and industry.

To digress, it is interesting to note that these documents were, for the greater part, written in Greek, though not exclusively so. A number of other languages occur, including Egyptian, that is, Coptic, written in a script based upon the Greek alphabet. But even after the end of the Ptolemaic period Greek was retained for legal purposes though it is suspected that only a small percentage of the native population could write it. Professional scribes existed who could be called upon when necessary (Turner 1968:82). Greek persisted in the face of Diocletian's efforts to replace it with Latin and even survived the Arab conquest, remaining in use until A.D. 705 when Arabic was mandated for all official business (Atiya 1968:84).

The second source that complements the textiles is representational art. Here can be seen depictions of decorated garments, many of them similar to extant Coptic textiles. Of special importance in Egypt are the wall paintings of the Monastery of Bawit, founded in the fifth century. This monastic complex provides a series of depictions of decorated textiles, largely in the form of garments (Clédat 1904). Some of the best-preserved of these murals have been transferred to the Coptic Museum in Old Cairo. Examples including ones with clear depictions of ornamented costumes have been published by Grabar (1966:174–176, 179–180). Small in scale, but useful, are certain book illuminations. Some show the placement of ornaments on garments and other textiles, helpful in light of the present fragmentary condition of the majority of the real textiles (Grabar 1966:193–217). Manuscripts believed by some scholars to be copies of Alexandrian originals of the period under study, specifically, the *Paris Psalter* in the Bibliothèque Nationale and the Joshua Roll in the Vatican Library are of interest in this connection (Morey 1942, ills. 60, 62, 64–65). Other illustrated manuscripts, the *Vienna Genesis* and the *Rossano Codex*, are postulated to have originated in Antioch, but the general appearance of the garments and their decoration is similar (Morey 1942, ill. 67–69; Grabar 1966:201, 207). Particularly notable is a miniature in the *Rossano Codex* showing the Judgment of Pilate. His judicial "bench," really a table, is draped in a cloth decorated with a pair of gilded busts, a reference to the contemporary custom of having two emperors reigning at the same time (Grabar 1966:207). In this connection it is interesting to note that woven portrait busts are found in the Coptic textile corpus. One in the Rietz Collection, number 39, represents the goddess Isis.

Roman and Byzantine paintings and mosaics often include representations of decorated textiles that can be equated with the garments in the Bawit murals, those in the Alexandrian and Antioch book illustrations, and with certain textiles found in Egypt (Grabar 1966: 101–217; Dorigo 1971). A rich assortment of decorated garments with a Coptic look appears in the mosaics of the Piazza Armerina Villa in Sicily. Especially striking are the garments shown in two floor mosaics, one very large, one smaller, which depict hunting scenes (Dorigo 1971:127–168). The depictions of decorated garments in the apse mosaics of the Basilica of San Vitale and the nave mosaics of the Church of Sant'Apollinare Nuovo, both buildings in Ravenna, Italy, merit study as well (Grabar 1966:158–164; Paolucci 1978: 58–65). Certain textile ornaments visible on the garments worn by the courtiers of Empress Theodora and Emperor Justinian in the San Vitale mosaics resemble ones in the Rietz Collection: specific examples are cited in section VI.

The third source is an edict promulgated by Diocletian and his associates in A.D. 301. In form it is a document that lists every commodity and service its compilers thought likely to be offered for sale in any part of the Roman Empire. Each entry includes the maximum price, stated in denarii, sellers could legally charge for particular items or services. The nature of the goods for sale range in size and significance from peacock feathers to draft animals, and the services are equally varied. The edict was intended to help stabilize the economy, which was in desperate straits after nearly a century of increasingly rapid currency depreciation accompanied by ever-soaring prices. Copies of Diocletian's Prices and Wages Edict, transcribed in Greek or Latin according to the locale, were evidently posted in marketplaces throughout the empire. Copies, none complete, have been recovered from various archaeological sites—Lauffer has published a list (1971:58–60). Fragments of a Latin copy of the edict were found in Egypt, the use of Latin recalling Diocletian's attempt to mandate Latin for official use in Egypt. Surviving copies were cut in stone, but there may have been others painted on walls or notice-boards, not to mention the official copies kept "on file." By collating the fragments, scholars have been able to recover sizable portions of the edict in both the Greek and Latin editions. Graser (1940) has published a restored text; another, slightly longer, has been published by Lauffer (1971). Both are incomplete, but additions to the text continue to be made: the most important for the purposes of this study is the fragment from Aezani that includes a list of looms (Crawford and Reynolds 1977).

THE EDICT is believed to have failed in its purpose: to control inflation. Some Egyptian legal papyri reflect the edict's strictures, according to Lauffer (1971:13, 58–60), but its overall impact, if it truly had any, was short-lived. Though it did not accomplish Diocletian's goal, the edict is nevertheless of absorbing interest. It is a lengthy document, so in modern times numbers have been assigned to its 32 main divisions or chapters for the convenience of scholars. Items in each chapter are numbered as

well: some of these differ in different restorations of the text. Unless stated otherwise, Lauffer's item numbers are cited here. Certain chapters contain fewer than 10 items, others, over 100. To date there are 486 entries that mention either textiles or some facet of their care or manufacture such as the cost of tools, labor, or raw materials. These entries appear in chapters 7, 12, 13, and 19–29.

Although the prices stipulated by the edict may have never prevailed, it is reasonable to assume that they indicate comparative values, especially where textile materials and qualities are concerned. Chapters 26–28 list garments and utilitarian textiles made of linen in order of their cost, starting with the most expensive. Linen goods were evidently produced in four or five principal grades or qualities. The first three grades were further subdivided by the place of manufacture or export: Scythopolis, Tarsus, Byblus, Laodiceia, or Alexandria, linen from Scythopolis being the most expensive in each classification, that from Alexandria, the least. The fourth or fifth grade, the cheapest, is specifically defined as being suitable for the use of slaves and the poor, for example, items 31, 69, 75, and 96 in chapter 26. Wool garments and domestics are listed in chapter 19. A less-structured listing is followed in the parts of this chapter that can be decipered—much of the chapter is missing. It is possible that grades of wool textiles were less standardized than linen ones. Their origins are certainly more varied.

The Diocletian edict helps to establish two significant points about the Coptic textile industry. First, textiles came from many geographical locations besides Egypt. Coptic textiles survive in the greatest quantity because special circumstances favored their preservation, not because they were a unique class of artifact for their time. The second point is the fact that Coptic textiles were produced to compete, in both price and quantity, with textiles from other parts of the ancient world. For this reason, they are unlikely to have been greatly different from standard types of textiles made in other places. Support for this idea is given by the resemblance of textiles found in Egypt to those depicted in the Roman and Byzantine art mentioned earlier. The decorated textiles in art could be taken to indicate that textiles similar to extant Coptic textiles were used in many places throughout the Roman Empire, not only in Egypt, and at least some of these may in fact have been made in Egypt. This country had long had a major textile industry, so there is no good reason to assert that the better textiles found in Egypt were all made elsewhere. As the historian Grabar remarks ". . . it is equally impossible to maintain either that none of the decorated stuffs in current use in the Roman Empire were imported from Egypt, or that all the deluxe fabrics unearthed in Egyptian soil were necessarily of local manufacture" (1966:323–324). For now, as a working premise, it will be assumed that Coptic textiles are at least closely related to, if not identical with, contemporary textiles used in other parts of the Roman Empire, and much of what can be said about Coptic textiles could apply equally well to textiles made in other textile-manufacturing centers of the period.

By THE OPENING YEARS of the fourth century, textiles were made for many purposes; the most important was undoubtedly the manufacture of wearing apparel. Throughout Egypt and the Mediterranean world, people of all classes including slaves dressed in clothing made from woven cloth. Some of this was woven by the women of the household, an ancient practice, gradually being abandonded in some areas but continuing in others, especially where there were large households (Forbes 1956:22–23, 231–232). In Egypt, in the first century A.D., and possibly later, one could have a weaver come to the house and set up a loom. Payment, according to a papyrus with household accounts, found at Oxyrhynchus, was in food and drink during the time spent working, plus a fee paid when the garment was completed (Hunt and Edgar 1932:420–425). Garments could also be ordered from a weaving shop; another papyrus contains a letter reporting the progress of such a project (Barns 1966:151–153). For the hurried, or those who could not afford custom-made garments, there were other sources. Many large Roman cities had guilds of rag workers who recycled discarded textiles into bed quilts and outer garments for people of limited means (Frank 1940:203–204). The edict, in the chapters cited, lists many ready-to-wear garments: undershirts; loin-cloths; outer tunics for men, women, and children; different types of cloaks and shawls; head coverings, and the like; also such niceties as handkerchiefs (chapter 27, items 8–28).

The common textile fibers were wool and linen. Other fibers were used for textiles as well. Silk garments are frequently mentioned in the edict. These were were far more costly then ones made from wool or linen, even of the best grades. Cotton has not been identified in the surviving text of the Edict, but references to the fiber have been noted elsewhere (Forbes 1956:1–80; Lucas 1962:147–148).

The basic garment worn by virtually everyone at this time was a straight-sided, loose-fitting gown or long shirt, put on over the head. This was a descendant of the Roman *tunica* (Wilson 1938) and is often called a tunic in the literature. It differed from its ancestor in that it commonly had sleeves, a feature the Romans of the Republican period considered effeminate. A tunic could be worn alone or with other garments over it, depending upon the weather and the occupation of the wearer. Variations abounded, depending upon period and location. The Edict lists an almost infinite variety of garments, possibly reflecting the diverse nature of the population of the empire in the early fourth century.

Next in importance were textiles intended for furnishing living quarters. The compilers of the lists for the edict evidently thought everyone should be able to afford such comforts as bed sheets, blankets, and towels—even slaves and people in the lower economic classes. Special inexpensive domestic textiles are listed in chapter 28, items 53–56 and 74. The domestic textiles intended for display, such as covers for dining couches and beds, were likely to be ornamented. Chapter 19 of the edict, items 6 and 36, explains how the price for such textiles was determined by the weight of the material and the dyes used. Patterned and colored covers for cushions and couches are mentioned in the *Deipnosophists* of Athenaeus, no doubt because they added to the aesthetic pleasure of a banquet (Gulick 1969:118–119, 120–121, 208–209). Napkins were an adjunct to fine dining. Pliny mentions napkins made of asbestos fiber that could be cleansed in the fire (Rackham 1961:432–433). There is even evidence for the use of tablecloths, principally depictions in art. A hand-

some fringed cloth, ornamented with gammulae, covers the table in a mosaic depicting the Last Supper in the nave of Sant'Apollinare Nuovo in Ravenna (Paolucci 1971:64). There are napkins shown too, draped over the raised ends of the dining couches. Curtains and awnings were available for door and window openings, to provide shade and privacy. Mosaics in Sant'Apollinare show a palace with a curtained colonnade and a private house with a door curtain (Paolucci 1971:63–64). Wealthy churches and major public buildings had, as part of their furnishings, matched sets of curtains (Gervers 1977:71–72). It is possible that curtains in churches played a part in rituals, adding another aspect to the importance of textiles in daily life (Gervers 1977: 68–70). Textiles would have served industrial purposes too. Egyptian merchants would have needed heavy coarse cloth to wrap bales of textiles and to make sacks to hold grain, as well as canvas for the sails of the ships that carried grain and other exports.

COMMON AS THEY apparently were, textiles were much more than decorative or useful additions to life in Egypt during the first millennium. Textiles formed a significant part of the economy (Walbank 1952). Weaving had been an important Egyptian industry for centuries even before the conquest of Egypt by Alexander the Great in the fourth century B.C. During the Ptolemaic and, later, the Roman period in Egypt, this native weaving industry was encouraged and developed. As outlined by Forbes with the help of the relevant papyri (1956:235–239), it is apparent that the industry involved a sizable part of the population, not only those functioning as weavers, spinners, or dyers, but also the owners of looms and workshops, dealers in textile fibers and finished textiles, and fullers. An extensive bureaucracy evolved, much of it intended to keep watch over the weaving industry, setting standards and, more important, collecting taxes. From the Ptolemaic period onward, the evidence of the papyri and the ostraka indicates that attempts were made to regulate almost every aspect of textile production. Weavers were expected to be licensed and their products were evaluated for quality and, in some places at least, taxed when sold.

W$_{\text{HEN}}$ E$_{\text{GYPT}}$ became part of the Roman Empire in the first century B.C., the bureaucracy begun by the Ptolemies was retained and enlarged, and increasing amounts of Egyptian textiles were exported, to Arabia and India as well as to different parts of the Roman Empire. Traders in the time of imperial Rome ranged over a wide area. The extent and complexity of their trade has been described by Wheeler (1955). Most of his observations are based upon finds of objects made from metal, glass, and other relatively durable materials, but textiles must have been widely traded as well, being easier to pack and protect from damage than, say, items made of glass or pottery. Literature reveals that in Roman markets every possible type and grade of cloth from rags to the finest linen were sold. Competing with the Egyptian textiles were textiles made not only in Italy but in other parts of the ancient world as well: Sicily, England, Gaul, Spain, Syria, Mesopotamia, and even India and the Far East (Forbes 1956:232–240). The names of over 40 textile-producing regions or cities can be gleaned from Diocletian's Edict. Tex-

tiles described as African or Egyptian appear on the lists (chapter 19, items 32, 35, 54, 68, and 73), as well as bed and cushion covers from Antinoë (chapter 28, item 46). Textiles from Alexandria have already been mentioned; they are listed 17 times in chapter 26, 3 times in chapter 27, 4 times in chapter 28.

For about 200 years after the death of Augustus in A.D. 14, the Roman Empire struggled to maintain the peace achieved by this emperor, signified by the closing of the doors of the temple of Janus in 29 B.C., and to maintain the borders of the empire. Various military and civilian actions did take place, but except for the revolts in Judea in A.D. 66–70 and A.D. 132–135, these were in areas distant from Egypt. While peace gave the necessary institutions of daily life opportunity to develop, existence for the majority of Egyptians was dull, filled with hard work and onerous taxes. Egypt was essentially the personal possession of the current Roman Emperor and a prime source of his income. As such Egypt was administered by impersonal officials whose main business was ensuring this income. Weavers, in particular, were kept busy weaving items that would produce revenue and equipment for the army— some taxes appear to have been collected in the form of military garments. Johnson has published a translation of a papyrus, dated A.D. 138, that concerns a requisition of garments and hospital supplies for the army in Cappadocia (1936:627).

Life was not all drudgery though. Private letters and other documents reveal glimpses of lives that included occasional pleasures and diversions. Among the papyri are invitations to parties and contracts pertaining to the hiring of dancers and musicians for these events (Johnson 1936:297–300).

Many of the documents are literary in content: poetry and the texts of plays no doubt intended to be read for entertainment. There is evidence in the Oxyrhynchus papyri to indicate that some of the residents there had literary interests and engaged in scholarly pursuits (Turner l963:84– 88). Egypt did produce a number of scholars during this period, the best known, perhaps, being Athenaeus and Plotinus. Other papyri are educational or informative and contain directions and recipes for a variety of processes ranging from magical to practical. One important papyrus, of special interest in the present context, contains directions for the preparation and application of textile dyes (Lagercrantz 1913:24–41; 200–232).

The existence of this particular body of written material indicates that, though most people may have conducted business with the aid of secretaries or public letter writers, a significant percentage of the population was literate (Turner 1968:82–88). This could have some bearing on the subject of the varied motifs found decorating Coptic textiles.

I N EGYPT, as well as in other parts of the Roman Empire, this relatively uneventful period came to an abrupt end early in the third century during the rule of Septimius Severus, A.D. 193–211. In 235, the civilian government of the Roman Empire collapsed, and between this date and accession of Diocletian in 284, the empire had approximately 16 emperors. The exact number is not certain. The reigns of most were brief and ended in violent death, sometimes at the hands of the emperor's own followers. Along with frequent changes in leadership went serious economic problems of the sort that Diocletian's Edict was intended to correct. Subsequent centuries continued to be characterized by power struggles between various military generals for the position of emperor. These struggles continued in the Byzantine period with unabated vigor and caused a good deal of distress to the general populace.

Some scholars think the contenders sought support from the members of different religious groups, particularly those with large or influential memberships. This theory is a matter of dispute, but it helps explain the severe persecutions of the later Roman Empire, not only of Christians but of other groups as well. Whatever their cause, the persecutions helped to create an atmosphere of unease and mutual distrust, and the period became as Dodds puts it, "an age of anxiety" (1965). This was especially true for Egypt, though other parts of the empire were not spared.

People who refused to abandon unsanctioned beliefs, in spite of pressures to do so when shifts in power occurred, often suffered for it. Punishments ranged in severity from minor restrictions placed on individuals, involving loss of property or personal liberties, to full-scale persecutions resulting in painful deaths for many. The social groups suffering from these often lethal attentions changed from time to time, depending upon the faith professed by those in power, pagan or Christian. Even when Christianity became the only religion recognized by the state, factions developed within it that led to confrontations sometimes resulting in bloodshed.

For Egypt, the end of these doctrinal problems came in the seventh century, the culmination of years of struggle between the supporters of the Monophysite doctrine of the original Egyptian

Church and their Melkite Byzantine overlords who followed the tenets laid down by the Council of Chalcedon (Atiya 1968:69–78). After a period of Persian domination—A.D. 619–627—and a second, brief period of Byzantine rule—627–640—Egypt was conquered for Caliph Omar by the Arab general 'Amr ibn al-'As and became a Muslim country. After this conquest Christians and others not of the Muslim faith were all treated alike, sometimes with favor, other times, not.

In spite of the troubles experienced by the general population during these difficult centuries, some Egyptians, generally those who could write Greek or Arabic or who had other marketable skills, were able to find places where they were needed and, to a degree, protected. This was particularly true for the greater part of the Fatimid period when a number of Copts held positions of trust. The nineteenth-century historian Ya'qūb Nakhla Rufaila lists eighteen Copts who served as functionaries under Fatimid rulers in such important positions as viziers, private secretaries, and chiefs of personnel (Atiya 1968:88 note 2). Many other Copts evidently lived through the severe changes and shifts in policy and rule that characterized the history of Egypt after the beginning of the third century. Among the people who weathered the numerous social storms were craftsmen, most especially weavers. Not only did weavers survive, some may have contributed valuable techniques to textile-making processes, or at the very least, weavers may have adopted, preserved, and later disseminated certain technical achievements. However, as the inheritors of two great weaving traditions, Egyptian and Greek, Coptic weavers were in an excellent position to make significant contributions to the weaver's art, and evidence provided by extant textiles indicates that they may have done so.

Egyptian weavers during the early Christian Era made contributions in several different areas, none too clearly defined at present, because of the lack of adequate comparative material from neighboring regions. First, according to indications found in the papyri and the Edict of Diocletian, Egyptian weavers may have developed methods for copying famous weaves and special kinds of garments originally invented in other regions of the known world. There is evidence, mainly the edict, to suggest that this was a recognized practice in antiquity and not necessarily intended to deceive buyers. The edict includes Nervic and Mutinian cloaks made in Laodicea (chapter 19, item 38; chapter 20, item 4) and a type of Gallic cloak made in either Ambianum or Bituriges (chapter 19, item 72). And all of the Alexandrian linens listed in the edict and mentioned previously are described as Tarsian, copies, it would seem, of the more expensive textiles exported from Tarsus itself. Earlier, in A.D. 138, the weavers of Philadelphia, according to the military requisition mentioned above, were expected to weave four Syrian garments from the best white wool (Johnson 1936:627). Later, this apparent ability to reproduce foreign textiles was to stand Coptic weavers who had survived the Arab conquest in good stead, making it possible for them to produce textiles of types pleasing to Muslim taste (Golombek and Gervers 1977:88). The names of many textiles and special types of garments have been recovered from the papyri, and at least some are suspected to have been woven in Egypt

(Johnson 1936:338). An example, sixth century in date, is a list of the belongings of one Theodosius, deceased (McCarren 1980:47-51). The writer of the list was careful to distinguish between garments imitating Antiochian ones and a hood known or believed to have been made in Antioch. The source of the five imitation cloaks is not stated, but Egypt is clearly a possibility. Of the 14 garments plus 5 other textile items owned by the desceased, only the hood appears to have been imported, the origins of the other textiles are passed over.

W E COME NOW to a more certain achievement: the extant textiles indicate that Egyptian textile designers evolved a large stock of design motifs suitable for weaving. These are particularly interesting in that they appear to have been at the same time both decorative and symbolic. It is possible that some of them may have been characteristic of popular foreign weaves. If true, this could help to explain the great variety of design motifs appearing on Coptic textiles. This avenue will be explored further when design sources and individual textiles in the Rietz Collection are considered. Some textile and other historians believe it possible that popular motifs were "published" in pattern books that were used by craftsmen working in all media (Gervers 1977:68; Levi 1947:8–10). However, part of the long apprenticeships served by weavers may have been devoted to memorizing and mastering the more complex designs. Also, some popular designs are quite simple in outline, and resemblances between, say, a pigeon or a dolphin done in mosaic and the same motif painted or woven may owe more to the selection of subject matter than to

copying a design from a book. However it was created and maintained, the range of designs is unquestionably rich and varied.

N EXT, and by far the most important contribution according to some viewpoints, was the early use of a foot-powered loom capable of pattern weaving; such a loom may have been the direct precursor of the counterbalanced heddle loom that appears fully evolved in early thirteenth-century Europe (Carroll 1985). Again, the lack, at present, of suitable comparative material from neighboring areas makes this theory impossible to establish beyond all argument. There is reason to believe that Coptic weavers had a part in the foot-powered loom's development though not necessarily in its original conception. This may have been the work of silk weavers in the Far East. Although major differences between Eastern and Western foot-powered looms and patterned textiles make direct borrowing seem unlikely, travelers' tales about the existence of looms worked with the help of feet could have provided the inspiration to experiment. There is also the matter of the treadle looms for cotton textiles developed in India, possibly, as long as four thousand years ago (Broudy 1979:105). Eventually, it may have been Coptic weavers fleeing Egypt and the problems that developed there in the wake of the Crusades, who carried foot-powered pattern looms to Western Europe early in the second millenimum of the present era.

From the foregoing it is apparent that the subject of Coptic textiles can be examined from several different vantage points: descriptive, historical, technological, and philosophical. For this reason, the information relating to Coptic weaving uncovered during the course of this investigation will be presented in seven sections. Section I details the technological background inherited by Egyptian weavers of the first millenium. Section II presents the available literary and archaeological evidence that can be used to speculate about the textile technology of the Copts, most particularly their looms, whether indigenous or borrowed. Greek and Roman sources perhaps used by the designers of Coptic textiles are discussed in section III. Section IV speculates upon the philosophical concepts that may have influenced the choice of the Coptic textile motifs and also speculates on the reasons for changes in the style, from realistic to abstract, of some motifs. Section V lists, in chronological order, events that directly or indirectly affected the lives of Coptic weavers and, ultimately, the form of their products. Some of this section repeats material mentioned in the previous sections partly to provide a means of quick reference and partly to demonstrate the relationships of events not otherwise brought out in the preceding text. A catalog of the Coptic textiles in the Carl Austin Rietz Collection of the California Academy of Sciences follows, comprising section VI. This includes commentaries on textiles with features, technical or thematic, of special significance. Section VII is a glossary of terms used here and in the literature cited that relate to Coptic textile technology and decoration.

# I. THE COPTIC WEAVERS' INHERITANCE:
## Ancient Textile Technology

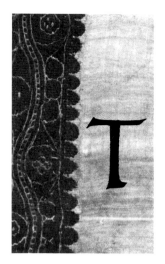

HE TEXTILE TECHNOLOGY that was at the disposal of Coptic weavers from the opening centuries of the Christian Era was, in large part, derived from practices evolved by the weavers of Dynastic Egypt before Alexander's conquest. The textile technology of ancient Egypt was based almost entirely upon bast fibers, particularly flax. Forbes states that the wild form of this plant has not been found in Egypt though it grows in neighboring countries (1956:27). From this fact it has been inferred that the flax used in the manufacture of the fragmentary linen textiles found in Egyptian sites of Neolithic date was introduced from outside (Lucas 1962). In subsequent periods flax was intensively cultivated in Egypt, and Egyptian linen became famous in the Ancient World. Pliny (19.2.13) observes that it was expensive (Rackham 1961:428–429).

The use of flax affected the direction taken by Coptic textile technology. The characteristics of flax are markedly unlike those of that other important Coptic textile fiber, wool. Flax fibers are strong and can endure high tension. They are smooth, hard-surfaced, and resistant to abrasion. When flax is being woven, the individual threads that make up a warp can be set close together, even touching, because they will be little affected by the rubbing of adjacent warps that occurs every time the shed is changed. Individual fibers of good-quality flax, properly prepared, are so fine as to be nearly invisible. Flax of this

quality can be made into yarn of such delicacy that cloth woven from it will barely conceal the wearer. This feature of fine linen cloth was depicted in Egyptian Dynastic art: female entertainers are sometimes shown wearing sheer garments that leave almost nothing to the imagination of the viewer.

These characteristics of flax must have affected the design of the looms used to weave linen textiles. The goal would have been the construction of a loom upon which could be woven textiles that exploited the unique qualities of flax fibers. As recorded in Egyptian art, this development took place in several steps. The earliest looms consisted of two beams to which were attached the prepared warp. The tension necessary to keep the warp evenly spaced was provided by pegging the beams to the ground with the warp stretched between between them. A drawing of this type of loom appears on a shallow bowl from a predynastic tomb at Badari, now in the collection of University College, London (Brunton and Caton-Thompson 1928:51, 54, pl. 48; Broudy 1979: fig. 1-8). Fragments of contemporary textiles have been found that indicate the kinds of textiles that were woven on this simple loom. Later depictions of Egyptian horizontal ground looms include more construction details. From these the presence of a simple heddle-rod can be postulated. Depictions of looms of this type in Middle Kingdom tombs, such as that of

Fig. 1. *A Middle Kingdom horizontal loom, shown in Egyptian perspective, with two female weavers seated on the ground working it. Drawing of a detail from the textile-making scene on a wall in the tomb of Chnem-hotep, c. 1990 B.C., Dynasty XII. Beni Hasan.*

the Vizier Daga at Thebes and Chnem-hotep at Beni Hasan, show a heddle being operated by two female weavers crouched on opposite sides of the warp (Broudy 1979:39, fig. 3-1). At first sight these pictures might be interpreted as depicting high-warp, that is, vertical, looms, but this is not so. Egyptian drawing conventions changed view-points in a single picture in order to show important details. This resulted in subjects such as tabletops, fish tanks, and low-warp looms, being drawn as if seen from above while other elements in the same scene may be drawn as they would appear viewed from the side. A detailed analysis of depictions of Egyptian looms made with these draw-ing conventions in mind has been done by Roth (1951:3–15). As further evi-

dence for their horizontal position, a model of a weaving shop found in the tomb of Nehen Kwetre at Thebes contains pegs that can be reconstructed as a horizontal loom (Forbes 1956:196; Broudy 1979:40, fig. 3-3).

Winlock (1922:71–74) assumed that the heddles on Egyptian horizontal looms were forced into position under the stretched warp by specially shaped wooden implement—heddle-jacks—that were knocked from under the heddle by the weavers, wielding hammerstones. The striking action had to be repeated every time the counter-shed was formed, then the jacks were replaced for the primary shed. If Winlock's interpre-tation is correct, the practice certainly indicates that the warp was under heavy tension. Otherwise the hammerstones would not have been needed to remove the jacks.

The tension on these looms may have been adjusted by removing a set of previously inserted laze-rods, one by one, as the weaving progressed. When all rods had been removed, it was necessary to pull up and reset the ground pegs and reinsert the laze-rods. Primitive in appearance, Egyptian looms of this variety must have been strenuous to operate. Nonetheless, linen textiles of high quality were being woven on them as early as the First Dynasty. The tomb of Zer at Abydos is said to have contained textiles with a count of 64 x 48 threads to the square centimeter (Petrie 1909:147), remarkable by any standard.

IT IS NOT ENTIRELY clear when the next step in the development of Egyptian linen looms occurred, but there is evidence to indicate that Egyptian looms of the Eighteenth Dynasty and later were constructed differently. Paintings in the tombs of Thot-nefer, Nefer-hotep, and Nefer-ronpet, all at Thebes, depict tall, vertical looms, built with rectangular frames constructed from thick beams, worked by men seated on backless stools (Roth 1951:14, fig. 9; 18, fig. 16B; 19, fig. 16A; Broudy 1979:46, fig. 3-11). It is thought that the Hyksos, a people of obscure origins, possibly with nomadic habits, intro- duced the vertical or high-warp type of loom when they invaded Egypt some- time in the seventeenth century B.C. When made in sizes appropriate for simple garments, small rugs, and blankets, these looms do not require side beams. The necessary tension is given the warp by suspending the warp beam from a tree branch or other sup- port and attaching the cloth beam to

pegs driven into the ground. This form of upright loom can be taken down when desired and rolled up, making it eminently portable. Upright looms of this same general pattern have been used by nomadic peoples in many parts of the world throughout history: the Navaho blanket loom is perhaps the most familiar today (Broudy 1979:70–75 fig. 4-8, 4-9, 4-10, 4-11).

In the hands of Egyptian weavers the upright loom evidently grew larger and more complex. Pictures of Eighteenth Dynasty looms show frames that appear to be free-standing but which in fact may have leaned against a wall or have been fastened overhead in some man- ner. Crossing the frame near the top was the warp beam, near the bottom, the cloth beam. Provision must have been made to move or rotate one or both beams, an adjustment needed to control tension and to allow the weaving of long strips of cloth. Exactly how this was done is not shown. Most likely, the tension was adjusted by slacking off one of the beams, which were held in place by cord lashings.

This was most certainly the type of loom seen by Herodotus during his visit to Egypt in the fifth century B.C. He observed and recorded in book 2.35 of his history that the weft on Egyptian looms was beaten downward, the exact reverse of the common practice of mankind (Godley 1975:316– 317). Herodotus noted another strange custom (or so it appeared to a Greek of the fifth century B.C.): Egyptian men, not women, stayed home and did the weaving.

An important feature of the upright Egyptian loom is its width. Judging from the size of the weavers shown working the looms in tomb paintings, cloth two meters or more wide could be woven on them. Two weavers working

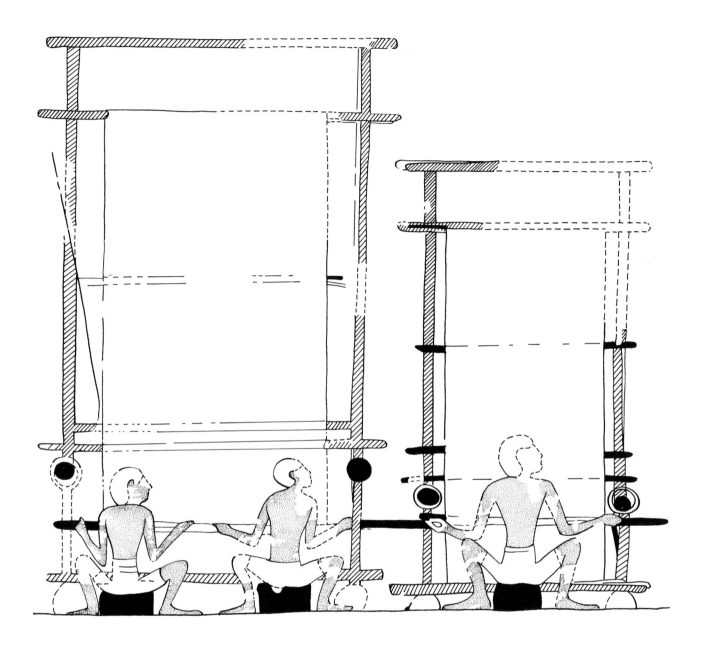

Fig. 2. *New Kingdom Vertical looms with male weavers seated on stools. The loom on the left is of exceptional size and is being worked by two weavers at once, a common practice for weaving wide textiles. Drawing of a scene on a wall of the tomb of Thot-nefer, c. 1425 B.C., Dynasty XVIII. Thebes.*

side by side are shown in some weaving scenes. Judging from some of the specimens of linen yet extant, long cloths—yardage, or several large garments—were woven (Roth 1951:14, fig. 9; 18, fig. 16B), further indication that the cloth and warp beams of Egyptian looms could be rotated in some manner.

An upright type of loom was inherited by Coptic weavers. They thus had at their disposal an excellent tool, well suited for the commercial production of fine linen textiles. Papyri of the first century of the present era provide

primary evidence for the survival and continued use of heavy upright looms into the Coptic period. Judging from descriptions in the papyri (Grenfell and Hunt 1899, no.264; Coles 1970, no. 2773), these looms were similar in construction to the earlier Egyptian ones.

Along with looms for weaving linen, Coptic textile workers must have inherited the technologies involved in producing flax and spinning it into yarn. The production of flax for linen weaving was well developed by the First Dynasty. Microscopic examination of the remains of seeds and fibers at sites in the Fayum indicates that the variety of flax grown earliest was *Linum humile* Mill., which was later renamed *L. usitatissimum* L. (Caton-Thompson 1934:49). All varieties of flax require good soil to grow well, but growing flax seriously depletes the soil, a fact well known in antiquity. For this reason, the Nile Valley with its annual flooding bringing new soil to the region every year was an ideal place in which to grow flax. Commercial production of flax in the Ancient World was undertaken only in places where land not needed for the production of food crops was available, often areas adjacent to large rivers.

From a description of flax raising and processing given by Pliny 19.3.16–18 (Rackham 1961:430–433), and supplemented by various aspects of linen production shown in Egyptian tomb paintings, it can be determined that the process was not technically complicated, but it was arduous and time-consuming, requiring many steps. It was, however, suited to mass production, and workers for many of the steps did not require specialized training.

Flax is an annual, grown from seed sown in well-prepared soil. When the plants are nearly mature, they are pulled from the ground, roots and all, a process shown on a wall in the tomb of Zau (Davies 1902, pl. 47.5). Next, the plants are made into small bundles and allowed to dry. Then the seeds are removed by drawing the upper ends of the dried bundles through a toothed device resembling a rake or a coarse comb (Newberry 1894, pl. 27). This operation, called *rippling*, is followed by *retting*. Retting consists of soaking the flax bundles in water for about ten days to two weeks (Newberry 1894, pl. 26). The soaking causes bacteriological

decomposition that makes it possible to separate the hard cortical tissue from the soft bast fibers. To make the separation, the flax is again dried, then beaten until the fibers are freed from the woody parts of the stalks. After a thorough combing to remove any remaining woody fragments and the tow—short, broken fibers never used for the most desirable grades of linen—the flax is finally ready for spinning.

The preparation of flax is still done by hand in many parts of the world (Hollen and Saddler 1964:40-41). Even when some mechanization is involved, the steps of the process are essentially the same as those followed by the Egyptians in the Dynastic period. Flax preparation methods are unlikely to have changed much by the Coptic period.

THE TOMB PAINTINGS make it possible to reconstruct the technique of Dynastic Egyptian flax spinning. These paintings have been assembled and studied by Crowfoot (1931:21–32). For the best grades of linen—that is, the thinnest and most closely woven—the fibers for the yarn were first made into a *rove*, a long bundle of overlapping, loosely twisted fibers that was rolled into a large ball. This ball was then placed in a wide-mouthed jar to keep it from rolling. Egyptian spinners used a type of spindle with a hooked tip and a hemispherical whorl set at or near the upper end of the spindle shaft. If empty, the spindle would have a short length of previously made yarn wrapped around it for a *starter*. The rove end would be attached by drawing a few fibers from the rove and holding them between thumb and forefinger of one hand, overlapping the fibers at the end of the starter yarn, and rolling them a little.

Fig. 3. *Egyptian spinners preparing different types of linen yarn. The female spinners on the right appear to be using two spindles at once, a feat possible only in the after-world, where spindles were, evidently, self-winding; the yarn magically wrapping around the spindle as it was being spun. Drawing from a scene in the tomb of Khety, c. 1980 B.C., Dynasty XII. Beni Hasan.*

The spinner then set the spindle twirling by rolling it quickly along a raised thigh with the palm of the other hand, allowing the spindle to drop after passing over the kneecap. During the seconds the spindle continued to hang and twist in the air, the spinner used both hands to draw fibers from the rove to feed the developing yarn. The gauge of the yarn was determined by the number of fibers employed, estimated by touch or feel and requiring a certain amount of experience. These fibers, held taut by the weight of the spindle whorl, were given the twist necessary to form them into yarn by the rotating spindle.

A length of yarn nearly equal to the height of the spinner can be made with one roll of the spindle. Some spinners apparently increased this by standing on a block or overturned pot. The method is shown in the tomb pictures of Baqt and Khety at Beni Hasan (Crowfoot 1931, fig. 8). When the spindle lost momentum and started to reverse its spin, it was raised and caught; then the new yarn was wrapped around it. Some spinners wind the new yarn over thumb and forefinger in a figure-eight pattern first, then rewind it on the shaft of the spindle to make a symmetrical packing. Egyptian spinners wound the yarn so as to form an inverted cone under the whorl. After placing the end of the completed length of yarn under the

spindle hook the series of actions was repeated, and so on until the spindle was full. It is important to note that, when done with the right hand, this Egyptian method of rolling the spindle on the thigh causes the whorl to revolve counterclockwise. This produces yarn defined as S-twist by textile specialists. Held in a vertical position, the angle of the twisted fibers slants to the left.

Like most pharaonic yarn, single-ply Coptic yarn is S-twist almost without exception. Elements of ancient Egyptian spinning methods survived in remote areas of Egypt up to recent times (Crowfoot 1931:31, 34–36). It is likely that Coptic spinners retained the technology of their Dynastic forebearers.

T‍HE USE OF FLAX as a textile fiber is responsible for another important feature of Egyptian textile technology carried over into Coptic weaving. Surviving Egyptian textiles of the pre-Christian era are commonly, though not invariably, white or pale yellow, the result of bleaching. Natural flax fibers are a gray-brown color. In Dynastic Egypt bleaching was accomplished by exposing the woven linen to sunlight for eight or more weeks, depending upon the thickness of the cloth. Forbes, in his examination of textile terms found in Egyptian texts, discovered several that refer to dyed linens, but these are few in number and generally late (1956:43). Undyed linen appears to have been the norm.

There are two explanations for this apparent preference for plain as opposed to dyed linen. One could be the fact that flax is a rather difficult fiber to dye satisfactorily with most commonly available, naturally occurring dyestuffs. However, a few colorfast dyes suitable for linen were known and used in ancient Egypt. Generally, dyed yarn was confined to a narrow stripe or two near the selvedges of an otherwise plain textile. Exceptions exist, but they are rare. Important examples have been described by Riefstahl (1944).

The second explanation that presents itself is perhaps the more believable. The majority of extant dynastic Egyptian textiles are from burials, a fact which may have had a bearing on the textile fiber used for funerary textiles. Sheep had been raised in Egypt in the pre-Ptolemaic period—Forbes states that flocks of sheep were pictured in Egyptian tombs (1956:4), and the regalia of the pharaohs in the Eighteenth Dynasty and later included a scepter shaped like a shepherd's crook. Certain Egyptian gods were personified in the form of a ram or as a human with a ram's head: Khnum, Harsaphes, and Amon of Karnak. Sheep wool was put to some use in ancient Egypt, for wigs, possibly, and coarse textiles for utilitarian purposes such as outer wraps to wear when the evenings were chilly. Wool cloth though, did not approach linen in value. Forbes notes that lists of gifts and offerings made to temples make no mention of wool textiles (1956:5). Wool textiles almost never appear in Dynastic burials (Lucas 1962:147). According to the observations of Herodotus, book 2.81 (Godley 1975)

the Egyptians considered wool to be ritually unclean, which would make it unsuited for wear during religious ceremonies or for burial purposes. Sheep tend to collect dirt and debris on their fluffy but naturally greasy coats which may be further fouled by excrement. This, and the fact that wool was commonly cleaned with the aid of urine, also an ingredient in some dye recipes, may have led the fastidious to avoid wool and dyed textiles entirely, given a choice.

It is surprising, then, in the light of a possible antipathy to wool textiles on the part of Egyptians, to discover that wool plays an important role in Coptic textile technology. Coptic weavers made all-wool textiles and also combined the fiber with linen. At some point wool became an acceptable textile fiber, both for ordinary wear and for burial. It is not at all certain when this took place though the Ptolemaic period is likely.

A solution to the problem posed by the change in attitude in the Coptic

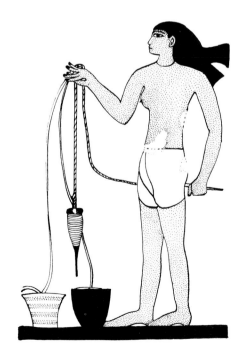

Fig. 4. *Another after-world spinner with two spindles; the second is held behind her, about to be set in motion. The suspended spindle is of the normal Egyptian form, with a domed weight, or spindle whorl, at the top of the shaft, and the finished yarn wound to form an inverted cone directly below the whorl. Spinners and weavers were depicted in Egyptian tombs to provide the deceased owners of the tombs with a never-ending supply of linen cloth, hence the need for magical spindles. Drawing of a figure from a textile-making scene in the tomb of Chnem-hotep, c. 1990 B.C., Dynasty XII. Beni Hasan.*

period is provided by the introduction of Greek concepts and customs into Egypt after the establishment of the Macedonian-Greek dynasty in the fourth century B.C. Except for the members of certain esoteric cults, Greeks had no bias against wool textiles. Textiles for everyday wear were either linen or wool, depending upon the weather or the season. Brightly colored garments were highly valued, judging from their frequent mention in Greek literature (Alexander 1978) and their occasional depiction in Greek art (Carroll 1965).

THE PAPYRI indicate that some early activities of Greeks living in Egypt not long after the conquest were directed toward improving the wool of native sheep by importing breeding stocks from regions famous for wool production. Special breeds of imported sheep were displayed in the festival procession of Ptolemy Philadelphus, described by Callixenius in a lost work, part of which was quoted by Athenaeus, book 5 201c (Gulick 1967:411). Three hundred of these sheep were Arabian, 130 Ethiopian, and 20 Greek, from the island of Euboea. During this same period, Ptolemy's minister of finance, Apollonius, owned a valuable flock of sheep imported from Miletus. Letters about these and other sheep have been preserved (Edgar 1926:3, 23–24, 57–58, 129–130). The minister's Milesian sheep wore covers to protect their wool, and their wool was harvested by plucking, not shearing (Edgar 1928:159–160).

Egypt was already the home of excellent weavers and the country's Macedonian-Greek conquerors' interest in sheep is an indication that they were not slow in taking advantage of this. All that was necessary was to induce the Egyptian weavers to use wool as well as flax to weave high-quality textiles, a simple matter, it would seem. However, introduction of a textile fiber like wool into a weaving industry primarily organized around the use of bast fibers does not occur overnight; no one knows how the change was accomplished in Egypt, or how much time it required. It could have happened fairly quickly. One important element may have facilitated it. Greece, like Egypt, had a long-established textile tradition. Furthermore, Greek women of all classes were expected to know how to produce textiles, if only to supervise others in the activity. Many of them wove, both for their own use and the use of their family, if Greek literature from Hesiod and Homer to Nonnos presents a reasonably factual picture of this aspect of Greek life. It is plausible to believe that the women who settled in Egypt with their soldier-husbands after the conquest of Egypt by Alexander in the fourth century B.C. taught wool-handling methods to their Egyptian servants and slaves while continuing to weave themselves. One of the female characters in the 15th idyl of Theocritus, written in the form of a short play, wears a new wool gown she wove herself (Gow 1950:110–111). It is interesting to note that she complains about the poor quality of the wool. The play is set in the third century B.C., in the reign of Ptolemy Philadelphus, mentioned above in connection with his imported sheep. Slave women, most likely Egyptian, though not specifically mentioned as such, spun Apollonius' fine Milesian wool in his factory in Memphis (Edgar 1926:3). All this suggests that, by the middle of the third century B.C., Egyptian textile workers had already become accustomed to handling fine grades of wool.

The chief loom of the Greek tradition

Fig. 5. *Greek warp-weighted loom. This famous drawing of the namepiece of the Penelope Painter was first published by A. Furtwangler and K. Reichold in 1932. It reconstructs details, principally the lower ends of the warps and the double row of loom weights, now flaked away from the surface of the original vase, an attic red-figured skyphos, c. 450–420 B.C. Chiusi, Italy.*

was markedly unlike Egyptian looms, either the earlier horizontal or the later upright variety. The Greek loom was derived from a totally different textile tradition, one born in Neolithic Europe. The early technology has been reconstructed by Vogt (1937), and its history has been brought up to the present day by Hoffman (1964). In contrast to the Egyptian looms, early European looms had but one major beam to which the warp was attached. In more advanced examples this beam could be rotated, thus serving as a cloth beam, making it possible to weave large textiles. There was no beam for holding the unwoven warp. In some times and places, warp for the planned textile was prepared by weaving a narrow strip or tape with an extremely long fringe of weft loops along one edge. These loops became warp when the woven strip was at-

tached to the cloth beam in a horizontal position. This unusual way of preparing a warp, which evolved in the Neolithic and early Bronze Age, has survived to the present day, according to Hoffmann (1977). It has been postulated that ancient Greek weavers used starting borders, but no firm evidence has been discovered. After the warp has been attached to the cloth beam it is divided into two or more sets of warp threads, depending upon the weave planned—plain or twill. For a plain weave, one layer will contain all the even-numbered threads, the other, the odd-numbered. The warp ends in each layer are further divided into groups, and each one formed into a hank to which a weight is tied. Some weavers may have wound the the warp bundle around the weight (Carroll 1983:98). Generally, antique Greek looms had nicely shaped weights of terracotta, some of them decorated. Stones or rough lumps of unfired clay have been used in other times and places. These weights are adjusted to hang a short distance above the floor or ground and impart tension to the warp and stability to the loom. For changing the sheds, one or more rod-heddles—the only type suitable for this form of loom—are put in place. Weaving proceeds from the top and the weft is beaten upward.

Starting at the top and working down is normal for netting and certain types of plaiting and twining, but it is not a universal weaving practice, though it seemed so to Herodotus. Because stone or terracotta loom weights are not readily destroyed by fire or prolonged burial, the presence of warp-weighted looms in a culture is easily determined, along with the dates of their introduction and, later, abandonment. Loom weights have been found in late levels in Egypt (Mace 1922–1923:75–76), but the original homeland of warp-weighted looms was Europe. There, they first appeared in the Neolithic period. From Europe the concept evidently spread both north and south, ultimately to Scandinavia and Iceland, but far earlier to the islands and the eastern shores of the Mediterranean. From actual remains and from depictions in art, it has been determined that a warp-weighted loom was the ordinary domestic loom of Greece from the earliest periods. It was most likely taken to Egypt by the Macedonian-Greek conquerors, specifically by female family members and servants. How extensive its use became there is entirely a matter for conjecture.

The appearance of Greek warp-weighted looms has been recorded by Greek vase painters. Eleven examples, dating from the early sixth century B.C. to the late fifth century B.C., have been

located and described by Carroll (1965:37–47). One of the more complete depictions, showing a front view of a double width loom, appears on an Attic black-figured lekythos in New York, attributed to the Amasis painter (Beazley 1966:154, no. 57). Clearly visible are the weights and the upside-down direction of the weaving (Broudy 1979:39, fig. 2-7). Because of its size, two weavers are operating the loom. The Pisticci painter included a side view of this same type of loom in the decoration of a calyx-krater (Trendall 1967:21, no. 53). His depiction shows the backward slant of the loom frame, necessary for the efficient functioning of the heddle, and the division of the warp into two layers, necessary for forming the sheds.

Experiments have demonstrated that weaving on warp-weighted looms is fast and efficient, and a variety of weaves can be executed upon them (Carroll 1965:48–51, 55). The remains of a warp-weighted loom set up for a twill weave were found at Troy in a house that had been burned around 2200 B.C. (Blegen et al 1950:349–354, 461). Warp weighted looms are admirably suited to tapestry weaving. The use of weights instead of a warp beam makes the warp unusually flexible. The individual warps are easily shifted and manipulated, a useful attribute when weaving a curvilinear motif.

After a period of experimentation with bast fibers in the Neolithic, warp-weighted looms were developed essentially as implements for making wool textiles, though upon occasion linen was woven upon them (Carroll 1973:366). To understand how this came about, it is necessary to consider the specific qualities of wool as a textile fiber. Wool differs from flax in many respects: it is less strong, and individual wool fibers are on the average thinner and shorter than the fibers of flax. One remarkable property of wool not found in flax is elasticity. Yarn made from wool will stretch under mild tension and will return to its former length when the tension is released. For this reason a wool warp needs less tension to keep it in order than a linen one. An important consequence, in the case of the relatively simple types of looms being discussed here, is that opening the shed requires noticeably less effort when the warp is wool, properly spaced, especially when a twill is being woven. Along with this property of elasticity are others that have both advantages and disadvantages that must be taken into account. Wool fibers have a rough surface, caused by an external layer of microscopic, overlapping scales. Wool warp threads must have space between them to minimize problems caused by the tendency of wool fibers to catch, cling, and even lock together when they come in contact. Making up for this disadvantage is the fact that the weft benefits from this characteristic, tending to stay where the individual shots are placed. This gives the weaver considerable control over the density of the textile being woven. If desired, the yarns of the weft can be packed so as to completely cover the warp, the roughness of the fibers keeping each shot locked to the last one. This is of special advantage when weaving tapestry. Furthermore, if an extremely thick, dense textile is desired, such as would be wanted for a heavy cloak or blanket, another special property of wool can be brought into play. When soaked in hot water, wool shrinks. Therefore, although a wool warp may be more open than is usual for a linen one, this can be changed, de-

Fig. 6. *Greek warp-weighted loom from an Attic black-figured lekythos. The best of the Greek loom depictions, it contains a number of significant construction details, such as the grouping of the warp ends and their attachment to the weights by means of metal rings. Attributed to the Amasis Painter, c. 540 B.C. Courtesy of the Metropolitan Museum of Art, New York; Fletcher Fund, 1931.*

liberately shrinking the dimensions of the finished cloth by washing it in hot water. Conversely, a textile intended to be have a delicate open texture would be woven from yarn that had been preshrunk so subsequent washing would not affect it. A letter mentioning this pretreatment of yarn, among other weaving matters, was found at Oxyrhynchus (Barns 1966:151–153).

Wool fibers have other advantages for the textile worker. The roughness and elasticity natural to wool allow the use of relatively short fibers for spinning. Preparing wool for spinning can be an easier process than preparing flax. Wool fibers can be spun in their natural condition, exactly as they come from the animal. Sheep grazing in areas where there are bushes and low-growing trees often catch and lose tufts of wool on

Fig. 7. *Seated woman preparing wool for spinning on an epinetron, a Greek device used to protect the thigh and clothing. Restored drawing from an Attic red-figured epinetron, c. 420 B.C. The surface of the vase is in poor condition, but the epinetron and the worker's hands, between which a roll of wool is to be imagined, are clearly visible. National Museum, Athens.*

twigs and thorns. Shepherds sometimes collect these tufts and spin them into yarn while watching over the flock. Raw wool is coated with a naturally occurring greasy substance which must be removed before the wool can be dyed. Some spinners prefer spinning wool with its natural lubricant left on, then washing the yarn to degrease it for dyeing. In antiquity wool was washed with a variety of naturally occurring detergents. Those mentioned in a third century recipe collection, the *Papyrus Graecus Holmiensis* (Lagercrantz 1913), have been identified as a soapwort, either *Saponaria officinalis* or *Gypsophila struthium*; a lily with an alkaline juice, perhaps *Asphodelus ramosus*; and two naturally occurring chemical compounds: colloidal hydrous aluminum silicate (fuller's earth) and sodium carbonate, also known as washing soda. Technically the process is called *scouring*. If the wool is to be dyed, it may be subjected to a second process called *mordanting*. Mordants are metallic salts used to develop the colors of some

water-soluble dyestuffs and to fix the colors permanently to the fibers. Common mordants in antiquity were potassium aluminum sulfate (dyer's alum) and copper sulfate (flowers of copper). Substances that may correspond to these are mentioned in the *Papyrus Graecus Holmiensis*. The actual coloring of the wool is either done at the same time as the mordanting or later, as a separate step.

V ARIOUS METHODS are used to organize wool fibers for spinning, depending upon the condition of the sheared fleece and the type of yarn, worsted or woolen, desired. Greek spinners in antiquity picked out foreign matter and snarls from the mass of fibers, added a little olive oil if the wool had been scoured, and hand-combed or carded it, shaping the fluffy mass of fibers into long, thick rolls. These rolls were compacted by stretching and compressing them between the palm of the hand and either the bare thigh or a special terracotta device called an *onos* or *epinetron*. This is shaped like a roof tile to fit over the thigh. The rove thus produced was wound on a short stick, the distaff, ready for the final spinning with spindle and whorl. Two women are shown preparing wool for spinning on the Attic black-figured lekythos mentioned earlier in connection with Greek loom depictions. With the wool preparers is a third woman spinning yarn from a rove that has been wound onto a short distaff. For the intermediate step of turning the roll (or rolag) into a rove, it is necessary to turn to a picture on another piece of pottery. This one is an onos decorated with a textile-producing scene that includes a depiction of a woman using an onos (Robinson 1945).
Greek spindles are unlike Egyptian

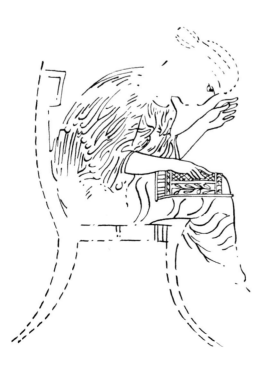

ones in that they have the whorl placed near the bottom of the shaft. The spinner twirls the spindle between the thumb and fingers, like a top, and drops it. While it turns in the air, fibers are drawn with one hand from the rove on the distaff held in the other hand. When the spindle is twirled with the right hand the whorl turns clockwise, producing yarn that is identified in the literature as Z-twist because, when held in a vertical position, the angle formed by the twisted fibers slants to the right, opposite to the normal angle present on Egyptian-made yarn. It is important to note, in this connection, that yarn with a primary twist in the clockwise direction is virtually unknown in Coptic textiles.

The Greek method of spinning was either forgotten or never used by the Egyptians; the latter is the more likely since their method would have worked as well for wool as it did for flax. Significant in respect to yarn twist is the fact that flax fibers rotate in a counterclockwise direction after being dampened (Newman and Riddell 1954). Linen yarn spun in a clockwise direction tends to unspin itself if it becomes wet. Cloth woven from Z-spun linen yarn is likely to develop a fuzzy surface after washing, rarely desirable. Wool, on the other hand, is not affected by the direction in which it is spun; there was no need for Egyptian spinners to change their tools or their methods for wool.

D OMESTIC SHEEP can be bred to have fleeces of several different colors: white, cream, gray, shades of brown, and black. All have been used in their natural state for textile production, but white or light cream are preferred for yarn or finished textiles that are to be dyed. Wool has a chemical composition that permits it to be permanently

Fig. 8. *Woman spinning wool(?) with a spindle, using a distaff to hold a supply of prepared fiber. Drawing of figure on a white ground Attic oinochoe by the Foundry Painter, c. 450 B.C. The form of the spindle is typically Greek, having the whorl near the bottom of the shaft, and a short distance above it a clew of yarn with a lentoid-shaped profile. British Museum, London.*

colored with a variety of dyestuffs derived from the vegetable and animal kingdoms. Dyeing can be done before spinning or weaving, or afterward. Dyeing the wool before spinning it results in more evenly colored yarn and may have been the method favored by Coptic spinners. Fibers of different shades and hues can be detected in many Coptic yarns when they are examined closely.

The dyes of ancient Greece and of all antiquity are known largely from descriptions of textiles in literature and from the writings of Pliny (Bailey 1925). From the latter it is apparent that by the first century of the present era dyers were able to provide a complete range of colors for the use of weavers. The dyes used included vat dyes, which require a number of steps to apply; as well as the easier-to-use substantive dyes, complete in themselves; and adjective dyes, which require a mordant.

THE EXTENT OF the contribution made by the Romans to Coptic textile technology is difficult to define. Roman expertise may have added to the chemical and industrial aspects of textile technology, the only parts that appear to have interested Pliny sufficiently to write about them. The Romans, like the Greeks, used the warp-weighted loom, beginning at an early period of their history; Seneca gives a fairly clear description of it (Gummere 1918: 408–411). Yet it was evidently discarded in the early years of the empire in all but remote regions. By this time the Romans may have considered the warp-weighted loom to be an anachronism. It was used only for weaving special traditional garments worn by brides for their weddings and by young men for their coming-of-age ceremonies. Even this use may have died out by the first century A.D., when the loom appears in the lexicon of archaic words and customs compiled by Verrius Flaccus (Lindsay 1913:364).

Depictions of looms in Roman art dating around this time show upright looms with two beams that are not noticeably different from those used in Egypt in the New Kingdom and later. Perhaps the best picture of a Roman loom is that found in a second-century tomb near Rome, discovered and photographed in 1913 (Bendinelli 1921:169–172; Broudy 1979:49, fig. 3-13). Broudy, while admitting that there are some strong differences between them, makes a good case for connecting the type of upright loom recently used in Palestine and Syria with the upright loom of ancient Rome (1979:48–49, fig. 3-14, 3-15).

Frank, in his study of the economy of Rome and Italy during the period of the Empire, noted an absence of literary and documentary evidence for textile-producing guilds (1940:201). Textile materials were produced in Italy, especially in the river valleys of the north. Spinning and weaving were done in some households, especially on estates, but not enough to account for all the textiles that must have been required by the population in general. By the early fourth century the Roman population evidently contained more consumers than producers of textiles. The long, varied lists of textile items published in Diocletian's Edict underscore the consumption aspect, while the many different geographical names applied to the various items suggest the importance of imports. It does appear that Roman taste could well have influenced the form and decoration of textiles made for sale throughout the Roman Empire.

COPTIC WEAVERS, then, had at least two, possibly three or more, textile traditions upon which to build their own textile technology. The basic foundation was formed, it appears likely, by the two well-developed textile technologies, Egyptian and Greek, which differ in almost every respect. Drawing from these, Coptic weavers were able to develop a new textile technology, which differed from anything that had been evolved earlier and which may have pointed the way toward the high level of weaving technology reached by the beginning of the second millennium.

# II. COPTIC TEXTILE TECHNOLOGY:
## The Literary and Archaeological Evidence

THE MERGING of the two older technologies of Egypt and Greece to produce an identifiable Coptic technology did not take place all at once, but details of the process are few, and interpreting them is a matter for educated guesswork. Important finds of early textiles, some with similarities to Coptic textiles, have been made in Syria (Pfister 1934, 1937, 1940; Pfister and Bellinger, 1945; Pfister 1951). Coptic weavers lived and worked in times of social transition, and such evidence as can be recovered suggests that their tools and methods of weaving were also changing. This latter point stands out clearly when the long history of textile technology is studied as a whole. Yet, at present, the details of exactly what happened to the art of weaving during this period of nearly a thousand years is not clear. What follows is speculative and invites challenge, and future discoveries will no doubt make changes and additions necessary.

There is precedent for determining the form of a loom from the textiles made upon it (Bellinger 1959). Therefore a beginning can be made with an analysis of the physical and visual characteristics of Coptic textiles. From the textiles it can be determined that the most remarkable Coptic weaving achievement may have been in the area of pattern weaving, though this marks a culmination, not a beginning, of the Coptic weaver's art. Patterned textiles, woven in wool as well as silk, and iden-

tified as being of Coptic manufacture, have survived, though not in large numbers (Trilling 1982:97–99, no. 108–111). These demonstrate that Coptic weavers evolved— or obtained from some place not yet satisfactorily identified— methods for pattern weaving quite unlike those used in China, a country in which silk was already being woven in patterns by the third century B.C. (Riboud 1977). Details of the evolution of silk weaving in the West are yet obscure and remain matters for conjecture (Trilling 1982:96, no.6). The extent of the Coptic contribution, if any, is unknown at present. Some scholars would have it that the development of silk weaving was in fact Syrian, but Wild has pointed out that this theory is based upon a single piece of evidence, late sixth century in date (1984). Chapter 19, items 9 to 19, of the Edict of A.D. 301 mentions silk and part-silk garments; the Edict also notes a loom expressly intended for weaving silk in chapter 12, item 32a (only in Crawford and Reynolds 1972:135). Wages for silk spinners and weavers are included in the Edict as well, in chapters 22 and 24. Silk textiles could have been produced in areas other than Syria long before the sixth century A.D., lending support to the original fourth-century date given to a type of silk textile featuring classical motifs that was first discovered at Akhmîm (Grube 1962:76). The one specimen of a silk textile in the Rietz Collection, Number 34, belongs to this group, being particularly close in appearance to certain examples published by Grube (1962, fig. 6, 8).

THE MOST CHARACTERISTIC and numerous Coptic textiles feature a mixture of two common fibers, linen and wool, woven in plain weaves; rep and tapestry. Forty-six specimens in the Rietz Collection are of this mixed-fiber type. These textiles were woven on an all-linen warp, and linen was also used for the plain areas between the ornaments. The ornaments, commonly bands, squares, ovals, or roundels, were woven in dyed wool yarn that completely covered the linen warp. It is highly probable that wool was used in order to have colorfast yarn for the ornamentation, not likely to run when the garment was washed. Pure white accents in the ornamental sections were woven in linen in the specimens examined. Usually the yarn was thicker and somewhat softer than that used for the warp and weft of the ground. The all-linen parts of the Rietz and similar textiles are commonly rep tending toward tabby, while the decorative wool and linen areas are tapestry, tightly woven and packed so as to completely cover the warp, virtually the exact opposite to the weave of the major portion of the piece.

Flax and wool, as already described in section I, have a number of contradictory characteristics. Combining yarns made from two very different materials in a single textile provides a challenge for any weaver, and it is a cause for wonder that it became so common a procedure in the Coptic period. The reason, already mentioned, was most likely the need for color. Coptic weavers evidently solved the problems created by combining the two dissimilar

fibers largely through patience and a willingness to improvise. Some of these apparent improvisations can be studied in the photographs of textile details, greatly enlarged, published by Du Bourguet (1964:8–16), as well as in details of some of the Rietz pieces included among the illustrations for the catalog section. Since the wool tapestry areas of a textile required widely spaced warps to permit the packing of the heavier and softer wool weft around the taut linen weft, ways to create such spacing had to be devised. In one method, the linen warp of the ground was regrouped, doubling or tripling the threads by hand and eye as needed, when the weaver arrived at the place where there was to be a decorative band or panel. This is clearly the method used for Rietz Number 8 where the disappearance of the weft in places allows the arrangement of the warps to be seen. Some of the smaller ornaments may have been worked by means of a coarse needle, as in darning. For large ones it would have been worth the trouble to install a special heddle. Another way of dealing with the problem was to skip over some of the warps, either cutting them away when the textile was finished or leaving them to float behind the tapestry woven areas. This latter method was used for Rietz Number 29, which still preserves many warp floats on the reverse side.

THE STRIKING appearance of Coptic textiles in their original state derived from the symmetrical placement of richly colored bands and geometric shapes on a plain, often white, ground. Textiles that have survived intact, or nearly so, make it possible to mentally reconstruct other, more fragmentary textiles, especially specimens not totally cut up. In the case of garments, the earliest extant Coptic tunics were ornamented with bands made of purple-dyed wool yarn. In the literature these bands are called clavi. When worn, the bands appear as vertical stripes extending from each shoulder, either to the waist or to the hem of the tunic, back and front alike.

This form of Coptic garment ornament is believed to derive from the insignia worn by Romans of the equestrian rank (Kendrick 1920:27). Tunics bearing such ornaments were originally woven entirely of wool, but the climate of Egypt and some other parts of the empire made linen the more desirable material at times. Coptic weavers wove both all-wool tunics and ones of a mixture of linen and wool. There are fragments of 25 woolen textiles in the Rietz Collection; the majority, it is surmised, came from garments. Some have designs similar to those decorating the combination textiles. In general the woolen fragments have a more uniform surface texture than the combination textiles because there was no need to regroup the warps in the decorated areas, and the entire textile could be weft-faced, not part-rep–part-tapestry as is the case with the mixed-material textiles. The basic types of garment ornaments persisted throughout, though designs changed.

The earliest bands may have been unpatterned. A few fragmentary textiles with broad plain purple bands have been collected; they are thought to be early, but their simplicity makes them difficult to date (Shurinova 1967, nos. 79–81). It is entirely possible that the shift to patterned bands with increasing amounts of linen ground encroaching on the patterned areas was evolved as an attractive method of making the expensive dyed yarn go

farther. An example of how this would work is Rietz Number 12, which has a solid band in the center and wide borders on each side worked in a formal vine pattern. From the Edict it is learned that part of the price estimate for a banded dalmatic (tunic) or other decorated garment was based upon the weight of the dyed yarn used. Commonly either a pound or a half-pound of yarn was used for the decoration of one garment, for example, items 12, 13, 15 and 16 in chapter 19. By working some of the yarn into a pattern with areas of plain linen background, a wider band could be created with a given amount of yarn than by weaving it as a plain, solid band. Labor was a factor, of course, but a pound (the Roman pound weighed 327.45 g) of wool yarn dyed with the best purple was expected to bring the seller as much as 50,000 denarii, chapter 24, item 2, while a woman weaver could be hired for 12 denarii a day, or less, including meals, chapter 20, item 12. Although some weavers, perhaps more efficient, were permitted by the Edict to earn as much as 40 denarii, chapter 21, 1a, the saving in materials would still be great enough to offset the extra labor that might have been involved in weaving patterned bands. (It should be mentioned that the Egyptian price system was based upon the drachma, not the denarius, and the two coins were not at this time equivalent; but this would have been taken into account if the legalities were being observed.) In any event, given the difference between the wages likely to be paid for the work and the high prices of materials, extending the area covered by a given amount of dyed yarn by working it into patterns seems a practical solution. There is also a possibility that patterned bands were a feature of garments with the half-pound's worth of dyed yarn while the solid bands characterized garments incorporating a whole pound. Some method for identifying the amount of yarn present in a particular garment must have been in use at the time of the Edict—otherwise its strictures make no sense. Many textiles in the Edict are described as *asemos*, (examples, chapter 19, items 3 and 11) meaning, in this connection, it is supposed, that they were without decoration (Lauffer 1971:262). The meaning of the word is "without mark or sign," the implication being that an item so described is without an identifying symbol of some sort. Perhaps the textiles did have ornamentation but lacked the symbol—a quality mark, as it were—that guaranteed the amount of expensive yarn present in the garment. This is admittedly conjectural, but could be a promising avenue to explore.

Whatever the cause, economic or changes in taste, surviving examples of Coptic textiles in all the known materials, early fourth century and later in date, are likely to have embellishments. Commonly, these are some form of tapestry, often worked with considerable finesse and comparing well with miniature tapestry textiles made by the weavers of other great weaving traditions such as that of pre-Columbian Peru. One type, not found in textiles made in other parts of the world, appears as a delicate linear pattern worked in extremely fine linen threads over a ground of plain tapestry weave. Examples in the Rietz Collection with this type of decoration are Numbers 1–10, 12, 14, 26, and 28. The technique has several different names, crapaud, ressort, or, misleadingly, flying shuttle or flying needle. Such embellishments have the appearance of embroidery, at

first glance, but analysis of typical specimens shows that the pattern was worked at the same time as the rest of the textile, not added later. The technique looks as though it may be related to bobbin lace. A group of bobbins that could have been used for the technique was collected by Petrie (1917:53, pl. 66). Three of them are made of ebony, the rest of a light-colored material, possibly bone. Bobbins of different colors would have been helpful in working intricate patterns. Baginski and Tidhar believe that the technique is unique to Coptic weaving (1980:261). A technique utilizing extra weft threads and sometimes mistaken for embroidery was known earlier in Egypt (Barber 1982). Included with ressort is another largely surface technique termed *soumak*. Coptic weavers used it to define lines too narrow to work in regular weaving.

Embroidery does occur on Coptic textiles, often no more than a stitch or two, done in order to refine or reinforce parts of designs otherwise rendered in weaving. Close examination reveals that some of the yarns of the warp and weft are split, evidence for the use of a needle rather than a bobbin or shuttle. Coptic textiles with extensive embroidered ornaments are known but they are relatively rare, and there are none in the Rietz Collection (Kendrick 1922: 56–68; Thompson 1971:27, 33).

Color is an important part of Coptic textile ornament, and dyeing must have been a significant part of Coptic textile technology. There is more certain information available for this aspect of weaving technology than there is for others. Until the late fifth or early sixth century it was fashionable for garment decorations to be essentially monochrome. At first the bands and rectangles were purple, though of varying shades, some verging on red violet. Dyes mentioned in the Edict are essentially those which yield these colors and which derive from various shellfish and from a lichen, possibly *Roccella tinctoria L.* The range of color variations possible is illustrated by the specimens in the collection, including an example of the more rarely used dark blue, Rietz Number 10. The tapestry technique was used to work floral motifs, mainly vine or ivy leaves, and the figures of men and animals as well as plain bands, squares, or roundels that served as the basis for ressort work. Beginning in the sixth century, according to some estimates, more colors were used in garment decorations though monochrome ornaments remained popular.

It is known that Greek textile workers had dyes for the full range of colors at the time of Alexander's conquest of Egypt. Some of these dyes are mentioned in Ptolemaic papyri. As early as the third century B.C. purple and saffron dyes were available ready-prepared in the form of dry powders sealed in packets (Hunt and Edgar 1932:412–143). Most dyes for red, orange, and purple were extremely expensive and so were restricted to luxury textiles. Everyday garments tended to be the natural color of whatever fiber was used. Substitutes for expensive dyes were sought for centuries. Some recipes, mainly those intended to replace the purple shellfish dyes, were collected by Hellenistic writers and preserved in extracts made in later periods. Eventually cheaper dyestuffs of satisfactory quality were found, and, as a result, textiles with colored ornaments became generally available. Chemical analysis of the dyes of extant Coptic textiles indicates that Coptic textile workers made use of dyestuffs that were, with one exception,

not known or used earlier (Pfister 1935; Forbes 1956:98–126; Lucas 1962: 150–159). The exception was madder, *Rubia tinctorum*, a plant long cultivated for its red coloring matter. After the Arab conquest, it was partly displaced by another red dye, made from a shellac-producing insect, *Coccus lacca*. Blue dye was prepared from indigo, either *Indigo argentea* or *Indigofera coerula*, which largely replaced the older dye plant, woad, *Isatis tinctoria*. Purple was no longer made from dyes derived from shellfish, but from various substitutes, including the lichen mentioned. Some of these substitute dyes may not have been particularly permanent. The dull brown decorations found on many surviving textiles may have been purple or red violet when newly dyed. Other textiles still display motifs worked in deep shades of purple that show no signs of fading or obvious color change, being the same color on both sides. These could have been produced by overdyeing indigo-dyed yarn with madder or lac. The same process of overdyeing was followed to obtain green or orange. For yellow, a good dye was prepared from *Rhamnus infectorius L.*, commonly called Persian berries. Possessed of a set of dyes in the primary colors, a good dyer could produce colored yarns in an almost infinite range of hues, and yarns of the extant textiles with their varied colors, many apparently as clear and bright as when first dyed, indicate a good understanding of dyeing on the part of the ancient dyers.

Once satisfactory dyes were discovered and methods of applying them developed, they tended to be retained for generations; changes only occured when certain dyestuffs became unavailable or new ones were discovered that were better or less costly. To a limited extent, dyestuffs, and the colors

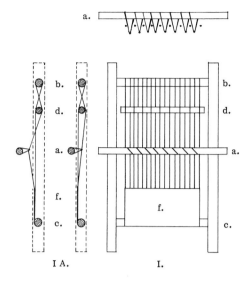

Fig. 9. *Diagram of a Roman upright loom derived from the looms in a relief on a building in the forum of Nerva, c. A.D. 98, and also from a loom shown on the wall of a tomb built near Rome, c. A.D. 175.*
I. *Front view of an upright loom set up for plain weave.*
IA. *Side view, showing the two positions of the heddle that form the shed and counter shed.*
a. *The heddle, a plain rod with cord loops, each attached to every second thread of the warp. The odd numbered threads float freely between the heddle loops as shown in the small upper diagram.*
b. *The warp beam.*
c. *The cloth beam.*
d. *The laze rod.*
f. *The cloth.*

made from them, can aid in dating Coptic textiles that were intended for garments: the more varied the colors used in a single piece, the later it is likely to be. The reverse is not true, however, since monochrome designs continued to be woven throughout. Early textiles other than garments are sometimes richly colored, but the colors approximate those in nature when the subject matter is figurative. Weavers of late polychrome textiles, on the other hand, often depicted plants and animals in the most improbable of hues.

Returning to the matter of the looms that may have been used, there is a certain amount of indirect evidence concerning them that can be helpful. The first looms used by the Copts could have been the relatively simple ones described in section I, used earlier by their Egyptian, Greek, and some Roman predecessors. These looms all had one thing in common: a vertical, that is, high, warp. By the beginning of the Christian Era, high-warp looms were in standard use throughout the Mediterra-

nean and adjacent areas and were certainly used by Coptic weavers for many of their textiles. Some of these looms may have been of the Greek warp-weighted variety, a point suggested by the possibly deliberate distortion of the warp plainly evident in early textile specimens. The extreme displacement of warp ends such as can be seen in Rietz Number 6 could be evidence for the use of a warp-weighted loom by Coptic weavers, at least for special types of ornamental weaving. The warp-weighted loom or knowledge of it, lasted well into the Coptic period. A fifth-century Egyptian writer, Nonnus, mentions warp stretched by stones in his description of Aphrodite's attempts to weave a shirt for her bridegroom, *Dionysiaca* 24: 253–255. A sad botch she made of it, too, until at last her fellow deities begged her to cease (Rouse 1940:240–247).

The construction of both of the principal varieties of high-warp loom, the two-beamed one and one with a single beam and warp weights, can be readily visualized with the help of loom depictions in Greek and Roman art. It is conjectured that there were differences between these looms and those of the Copts because weavers in general tend to develop localized ways of setting up looms and working them. Such differences are unlikely to have been very great.

From legal documents of the first century A.D. that mention and describe looms, it is learned that what may have been the common loom was approximately 1.5 meters wide and consisted of an upright frame constructed from four beams (Grenfell and Hunt 1899:234, no. 264; Coles 1970:65, no. 2773).

For about 1000 years there are no significant depictions of looms in Mediterranean or European art. Then,

Fig. 10. *Medieval English horizontal harness loom. Drawing from a photograph of a page of an illuminated manuscript showing a weaver at work. In position the loom has gone full circle, and is back to being horizontal again, this time with legs to bring it up to a comfortable working level. The heddle mechanism is explained in figure 11. Trinity College, Cambridge.*

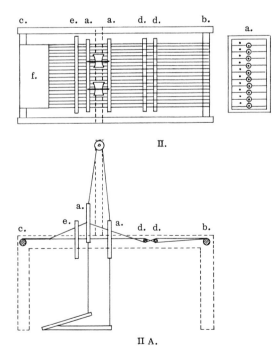

Fig. 11. *Diagram of a Medieval English loom, as shown in fig. 10.*
II. *Top view of loom set up for plain weave.*
IIA. *Side view of loom showing the open shed and the treadles attached to the heddles. Opening the counter shed is done by depressing the raised treadle.*
a. *The heddles. They are suspended by cords running over spool-shaped pulleys threaded on a round rod which in turn is supported by vertical supports attached to the side beams of the main body of the loom (shown as dotted lines in IIA). A cord and a simple treadle is attached to each heddle,*
*making it possible to change their position, and the shed. One heddle controls the even numbered warp threads, the other, the odd. Every thread passes through an eyelet of the heddle that controls it, and between the cords or wires that hold the eyelets of the opposite heddle, as shown in the small diagram to the right of II.*
b. *The warp beam.*
c. *The cloth beam.*
d. *The laze rods.*
e. *The reed beater, used to compress the warp and guide the shuttle. Not suited for use on upright looms, hence absent from the diagram of loom in fig. 9.*
f. *The woven cloth.*

in the late thirteenth century, scenes of textile making reappear in art. Perhaps the earliest of this new generation of pictures is one in an illuminated book now at Trinity College, Cambridge, MS. 0.9.34 fol. 32b (Cipolla and Birdsall 1979:82; Broudy 1979:141, fig. 8-4). It shows a weaver working at his loom, producing a textile with a lozenge pattern. The forms of the looms in book illustrations of this period and later offer surprises. Most are radically different from any looms represented earlier. The medieval looms are generally shown with a horizontal warp held in a frame so as to be about a meter above the ground or floor level. The heddle leashes are no longer attached to a simple rod, but are instead stretched in two rectangular frames suspended from pulleys. Perhaps the most remarkable features of these looms are the treadles, one for each heddle frame, that allow the shed to be changed with the feet, leaving both hands free to insert the weft and beat it into place.

This change in loom type was both marked and lasting: looms nearly identical in form are still in use. The working principle of these looms is so unlike that of the looms of antiquity that it is certain something quite remarkable happened to weaving technology in the thousand years that elapsed between the latest clear illustration of an ancient loom and the earliest one of a modern loom. A veritable mystery, yet in spite of the apparent difficulties the matter is one that requires an attempt at solution. The problem of the Coptic looms is central to the question of the origin of the horizontal or low-warp looms that we first find in use by Medieval European weavers. It has never been precisely determined when the old high-warp looms of the Near East were largely replaced with the treadle-operated low-warp looms. Such evidence as can be found indicates that the change may have been instigated by Coptic weavers, though perhaps with inspiration provided by outside sources. Establishing a date for this event, even an approximate one, should help to clarify the early history of one of the most significant of all inventions, a foot-powered loom that freed both hands to manipulate the weft. Of even greater importance, it should also help to refine and clarify the history of weaving in Egypt after the Ptolemaic period and the history of weaving in the eastern Mediterranean countries in general.

Some help in answering this question might be expected from archaeological remains. A few ancient loom parts and weaving accessories were collected by the Egyptologist Petrie. A particularly intriguing specimen is a boat shuttle (Petrie 1917:127, pl. 66). The shuttle is typical of the kind that was developed for weaving on low-warp looms with frame heddles and thus constitutes possible evidence for the existence of these looms in Egypt. Unfortunately Petrie's shuttle lacks a provenance, and it may not be Egyptian at all, let alone ancient. Roth corresponded with Petrie about his boat shuttle (1951:148 n. 2.) and learned that Petrie had bought it, not excavated it. In Roth's opinion it was "an eighteenth-century English shuttle with exotic decoration."

It is a disapointment that this shuttle cannot be verified as to age and origin because the existence of such an object in Egypt during the Coptic period would be of great help in establishing the presence of a low-warp, foot-powered loom. However, boat shuttles are normally used with another important loom accessory, the *reed*, an essential feature of developed low-warp looms, though not necessarily ones worked with the help of the feet. The reed keeps the warp evenly spaced and is mounted so it can be drawn quickly toward the weaver and the evolving web, packing the weft solidly in place with one quick gesture rather than resorting to a series of whacks as is done when compressing the weft with a weaver's comb or a sword beater. When the shuttle is thrown from one hand to the other through the open shed, the reed also serves to guide the shuttle as it glides over the lower layer of the warp. Like the boat shuttle, the reed is an adjunct of the low-warp loom only; neither accessory has a place in weaving on a vertical warp. Because the two tools are used in conjunction, the presence of one or the other can be taken as virtually certain evidence for the existence of both.

Archaeological evidence for the reed is more plentiful than for the boat shuttle. Three reeds identified as Coptic have been found in Egypt (Roth 1951: 24–26). Their measurements and construction details are as follows:

1. 68.6 cm long, reeds made of cane or wood, seven to the centimeter
2. 73.7 cm long, reeds made of cane or wood, eight to the centimeter
3. 66 cm long, flat iron reeds, count not stated.

Numbers l and 2 were found in an empty tomb near Abu Kurkas; the provenance of number 3 is not given and may be unknown. All three lack associated remains, consequently their exact dates are open to question.

A weaver working a low-warp loom most commonly does so in a seated position. Weavers using a high-warp loom may or may not sit while weaving except for warp-weighted looms, which are more readily worked while stand-

ing. These points are to be kept in mind when considering the next scrap of evidence. Artemidorus of Ephesus mentions both a vertical and a horizontal type of loom in his *Oneirocritica*, written in the second century A.D. (White 1975:167). In his third book he states that to dream of an upright loom, ". . . signifies movements and trips abroad, since a woman who plies this loom must go back and forth. A horizontal loom is a symbol of delay, since the women who ply this loom are seated." While there is nothing to indicate that this horizontal loom was anything more elaborate than a version of the regular two-beamed vertical loom placed horizontally and set on legs like a table, it may indicate an early step in the evolution of the foot-powered loom. Both types of loom must have been fairly common at the time to figure in a book of this nature, the interpretation of dreams.

DATED EVIDENCE for foot-powered looms was discovered at the site of the Coptic Monastery of Epiphanius at Thebes in Egypt. Here, excavators uncovered eight brick-lined depressions, each constructed with a ledge at one side near the top (Winlock 1926–1933:68–69). They were located in different areas throughout the site, generally near doorways, perhaps for the sake of the light. It has been postulated that these were pits for single-treadle, low-warp looms, operated by a weaver who sat on the ledge—really a built-in seat. Associated finds, pegs, holes, cord fragments, abraded places, and, in some of the pits, what could be treadle fulcrums, provide evidence for this identification. All but one of the pits appeared to be intended for narrow looms such as would be used to weave

Fig. 12. *Diagram illustrating two ways of weaving a full-length, 1.3 m. Coptic tunic with tapestry bands ornamenting the sleeves and shoulder areas. The parallel lines represent unwoven areas of the warp. A. Weaving a full length tunic in one piece requires a loom capable of holding a warp with a width equal to twice the length of the completed garment. Weavers may have avoided wasting warp yarn by putting the warp for the sleeves on first. The rest would be added after the first sleeve had been completed and wound on the cloth beam, perhaps only enough for the body of the tunic. While possible to do on a regular two-beamed loom, the method would have been better suited for a warp-weighted loom of the type shown in figs. 5 and 6. B. Weaving a tunic on a warp half as wide, and with little waste of warp or need for special manipulations, can be done by weaving the sleeves separately and the body as a wide rectangle with a slit for one armhole. The completed garment will have seams over the shoulders and but one side seam.*

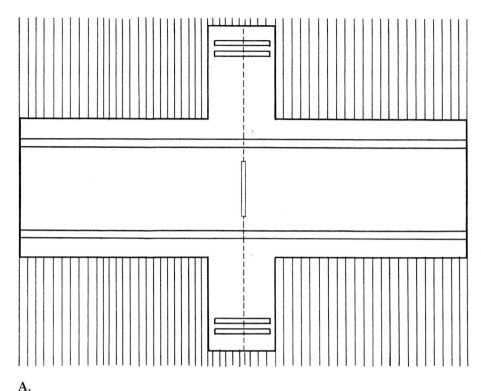

A.

B.

bands or tapes. The excavators concluded from the pits and associated remains that a simple harness loom with one treadle for changing the shed was known in Egypt by the early seventh century, a view supported by Usher (1954:54).

The origin of this type of loom is disputed. One possibility takes into account the pit-treadle looms used by the cotton weavers of India, suspected by some to be extremely ancient, perhaps existing in a recognizable form as long as 4000 years ago (Broudy 1979:105). Egypt did trade with India during the Roman period, and Egyptian weavers could have learned about heddles worked with the feet, if only by hearsay. The pit-treadle form postulated for these Epiphanius looms was used in East Africa during the nineteenth century (Roth 1950 62–63). While it may be presumptuous to assume that these represent a survival of the Egyptian version of a pit loom—too many outside influences have had the time to disturb any orderly historical sequence—some of these later looms, which lack heavy elaborate frames, may give an idea of how the earlier looms were set up.

A different class of evidence indicates that low-warp, possibly treadle looms may have been developed considerably earlier than the seventh century. This evidence consists of whole or restorable textiles. Some of these were perhaps made upon the looms in question, others, as will be made clear, were most certainly not. An important clue in determining the type of loom used is the size of the completed textile. Certain of the looms used by Coptic weavers must have been quite large. One curtain, perhaps found at Akhmîn but now in the Royal Ontario Museum, is an impressive 2.32 m wide (Gervers 1977:56). Even more imposing are some Coptic garments, most importantly the long, full tunics worn by adults. The fact that wide looms were needed for the finest early Coptic tunics is not immediately obvious to nonweavers, so a slight digression on tunic design is in order.

THE EXTERNAL appearance of the full tunics worn by Copts from the fourth century to the mid-seventh, when they went out of fashion, remained essentially unchanged, except in the ornamentation of the individual decorative elements. Garments of this type were not peculiar to Egypt but were worn throughout the Roman Empire. It is believed that these tunics, called *dalmatics*, were introduced to Rome by the Emperor Elagabalus early in the third century. Sleeved tunics had been common garments in the Near East for many centuries previously, but the classical peoples of the Mediterranean were slow to adopt the fashion; some,

the Romans in particular, were conservative in matters of dress. The name dalmatic derives from Dalmatia, where the garment had long been in general use (Norris 1949:43).

While dalmatics were made specifically for men, women, and children— information derived from the Diocletian Edict—there seemed to be a one-size-fits-all attitude shown in their manufacture. Some specimens have had deep horizontal tucks sewn into them, evidently for the purpose of adapting them to a short wearer (Thompson 1967:84, no. 37; Trilling 1982:77, no.74). A regular tunic could be shortened by belting it and drawing up the excess, but dalmatics were customarily worn unbelted. Though representations in art show that men's and women's dalmatics were similar in appearance, women's cost more, according to the Edict, even for the same type and quality. They may have been cut fuller to obviate buying maternity garments. Any dalmatic, however, was essentially a quality garment, if for no other reason than the amount of cloth required to construct one.

The persistence of this form of tunic for centuries—versions of it have lasted even to the present day for ecclesiastical and academic robes—has caused one extremely important point to go unnoticed. The tailoring, if the term is appropriate for the construction of unfitted garments, changed as time passed. These changes can be most readily recognized by identifying the number of pieces used to construct a particular tunic. Some of the earliest tunics that have survived more or less complete are remarkable for having been made entirely in one piece, sleeves and body, including ornament. The ornamentation was fairly standard and has been diagrammed by Start (1914: 33–35), Lewis

*Fig. 13. Coptic tunic design schemes that incorporate varieties of tunic ornaments present in the Rietz collection.*

*Scheme I is the basic scheme. Stripes, called clavi, cross over the shoulders, running from hem to hem. Similar stripes, narrower and doubled, decorate the sleeves. Rietz Number 5 may be part of a tunic that followed this design scheme, as may Number 2. In a minor variation, small insets were placed on the upper sleeves. Specimens of suitable insets are Rietz Numbers 9 (now sewn to a veil), 14, 17, and 18. Of the many possible variants upon this basic scheme of clavi and sleeve stripes, the most common utilizes half-length clavi. In schemes II and III ornaments of various shapes are placed below the ends of the clavi on the lower half of the garment. The sleeves have matching insets and the usual double stripe at the wrists. Tunics classified as scheme II tend to have ornaments that are larger and more colorful than those appearing on scheme III tunics, with more of the*

*ground covered by the decoration. Rietz Number 3 is almost certainly from a decorated tunic of this type, and quite possibly Number 21, which is figured. The clavi might be figured too, and richly colored as in Rietz Number 42. The half-length clavi of scheme III tunics are commonly narrower and often delicately patterned. The clavi may have round, pointed, or leaf-shaped terminations. There are several good examples of scheme III ornaments in the Rietz collection: Numbers 19, 20, 48, and 56. Scheme IV is an elaboration of I, more often than not having full-length clavi. The space between the clavi immediately below the neck opening is filled with patterned bands, figured bands, or an elaborately decorated panel. Shoulder insets might be woven as side extensions of the clavi ar placed apart. Pieces of scheme IV tunics in the Rietz collection are Numbers 13, 31, 35, 55, and 65. The sleeve bands are likely to be wider and more elaborate than in the other schemes described here.*

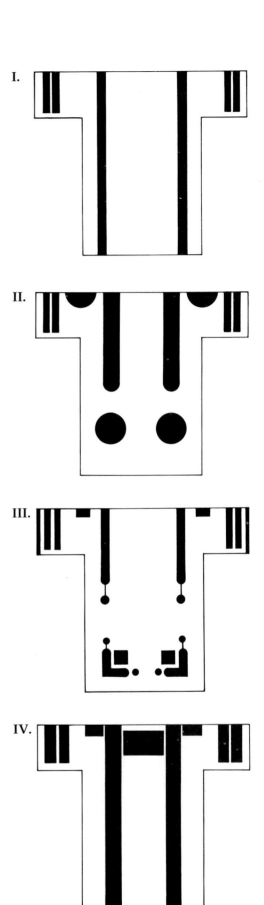

I.

II.

III.

IV.

(1969:9), Thompson 1971:4–5), and others. There is usually a single broad stripe running over each shoulder, smaller matching stripes, often doubled, on the sleeves, and squares or roundels on the shoulders and in the vicinity of the knees. Most or all of the ornamentation was woven concurrently with the ground, but, as mentioned earlier, in a different weave when the textile was a combination of linen and wool. Then the ornaments were woven in tapestry, a weft-face weave, while the ground was woven in rep, a warp-faced one.

Combining these particular weaves created problems for the weaver. In order to weave the garment in one piece with the warp running in the correct direction for the tapestry ornament, the textile had to be woven on a loom close to three meters wide. One early tunic, preserved entire, measures 2.59 m from one hem selvedge to the other. It is now in the Victoria and Albert Museum (Kendrick 1920, no. 1, pl. 1). To construct such a garment, a sleeve would be woven first, then the body of the tunic with a vertical slit for the head in the center, then the second sleeve. Laid flat, the unsewn tunic had the form of a cross with two wide, thick arms and two short, thinner arms. When completed, a tunic of this one-piece pattern would have a seam on each side running under the arms and a distance down the sides—some wearers evidently preferred to leave the side seams partly or entirely open—but no seams elsewhere. (A needleworker, it is learned from Diocletian's Edict, might earn from 4 to 6 denarii for sewing or otherwise completing a garment, chapter 7, items 48 and 51.)

The width of the loom needed for these large textiles, both curtains and garments, makes it unlikely that the looms used were low-warp, treadle-operated looms equipped with a reed beater. Either such looms had not yet become common at the date when these textiles were made, or the older loom was retained for large textiles much as the warp-weighted loom, according to Verrius Flaccus, had been retained by the Romans for ceremonial garments.

Eventually changes were made in the basic one-piece design. The sequence is not defined and the dates when the different types were made may have, in fact, overlapped. The process could have begun as early as the late fourth or early fifth century. By this time tunic sleeves were sometimes woven separately and sewn on when the garment was completed. The body of the garment was still an elongated rectangle woven horizontally and with a vertical neck slit. About the middle of the fifth century changes became even more marked. Instead of the poncho construction with a neck slit, the body of the tunic was constructed from a square of material folded in half and sewn up one edge, forming a tube to which separate sleeves were attached by sewing. There is an example of a tunic made to this pattern in the British Museum (Start 1914:33, fig. 34). The ornamental shoulder bands were still woven in tapestry, but the loom needed to be only half as wide as formerly. Material for tunics made according to this pattern could readily be woven on a low-warp harness loom, even a relatively narrow one, although similar tunics could have been produced on upright looms as well.

Exploring the problem further, though, it is necessary to consider the following. Unless it is desired to weave a wall hanging or other large textile, harness looms have significant advantages over upright looms. An important one in this instance is the greater weaving speed that can be achieved, particularly when the width of the finished cloth is a meter or less. By changing the pattern of the tunic to a three-piece version, several tunics could be made in the time it would take to weave a single one-piece garment. Several tunics could be woven on a single warp, an adaptation that has economic advantages. The narrower warp took no more than half the time to prepare for weaving, even though it might be over twice as long for each tunic planned. There was little or no waste of warp because none of it had to be left bare on either side of the sleeve portions.* Only one weaver was required, and this weaver could work sitting down and remaining in place. Pairs of weavers sometimes worked high-warp looms; a single weaver was forced to move back and forth with each shot, a procedure both tiring and time-consuming. Further, increasing the efficiency of the weaver working at a low-warp loom, the shorter passage of the weft through the shed permitted the use of a weighted shuttle of special design that could be be propelled, or thrown, from hand to hand with a minimum of arm and body movement. The invention or adoption of suspended

harness frames that could be activated by the feet made weaving even faster.

Encouraged, perhaps, by the economic advantages, more changes were made in the basic tunic pattern. In another variation ornaments were woven separately and stitched in place on a completed garment, commonly one of the three-piece variety. This permitted the weaver to have the weft direction parallel to the hem of the garment if so desired, and a much narrower textile could be utilized for the main part of the tunic than was required earlier. Sewing the ornamental portions on as appliqués instead of weaving them at the same time as the ground was not a major innovation; it had been done from the beginning, usually in order to salvage the decorated portions of a worn-out or damaged garment. The move to appliquéd ornaments permitted specialization. Weavers with special talent or skill could devote all of their time to the production of ornaments, while others could carry out the less demanding mechanical aspects of textile making. Something of this tendency in the direction of specialization appears in the descriptions of textile workers in the Edict of Diocletian in chapter 20.

One piece of evidence that could indicate the relatively early appearance of a low-warp heddle loom in Egypt is a bill of sale. In A.D. 298, a woman named Apollonia purchased a second-hand loom. The bill of sale describing this transaction, Oxyrhynchus 1705, contains significant information about the loom that was sold, including its size: 6 cubits wide and 10 cubits long (Hunt and Edgar 1932:106–109). The unit of measurement is the Greek or nearly identical Roman cubit, the pekhus (πῆχυς), roughly equivalent to 45 cm. The loom,

---

* In a private communication, dated January 5, 1987, about Carroll 1985, Marta Hoffman has drawn attention to a Coptic tunic belonging to the Kunstindustrimuseet in Copenhagen, Denmark, with well-preserved selvedges. It shows how one weaver, at least, solved the problem of avoiding yarn waste, though at a cost of additional work. Hoffman states, "the tunic was set up with a starting edge at the sleeve and new starting edges show that the body of the tunic was started only after the sleeve had been completed (and presumably rolled up on a beam). The finishing seems to have been done accordingly."

then, was approximately 2.7 m by 4.5 m. Mentioned, but not described, are the loom's accessories or fittings. It is tempting to believe that these were heddle frames, a reed beater, and perhaps several boat shuttles. The sale record states that the loom was for Tarsian weaving, presumably a type of textile developed in Tarsus and, according to the Edict, made of linen and woven in Alexandria as well as in Tarsus. The price agreed upon by both parties totalled 13,000 drachmas, paid in the form of two talent's weight of silver and 1,000 imperial silver drachma coins. If the coins were of the pure silver coinage issued by Diocletian after A.D. 292, the total weight of silver involved was in excess of 334 troy ounces. For comparison, one of the first-century looms mentioned earlier (Grenfell and Hunt 1899; no. 264) cost a mere 20 silver drachmas, drachmas which must have been the severely debased coinage of the time of Nero.

Some idea of the value of Apollonia's purchase can be obtained by comparing it with an Egyptian weaver's wages and the prices paid for textiles. An approximately contemporaneous document, Oxyrhynchus 725, an apprenticeship agreement, reveals that a weaver with five years training could expect to earn 24 drachmas a month. Part of an apprentice's pay was in the form of garments, from which it can be learned that tunics for everyday wear ranged in value from 16 to 32 drachmas (Hunt and Edgar 1932:42–43). It appears that Apollonia would have had a long wait before her investment returned a profit if these facts have any bearing on the price she paid for the loom. They may not have: prices for tunics in the Edict are nearly all much higher. These prices may be greatly inflated. However, it is unlikely that this was a common type of

loom intended for utilitarian textiles. It is entirely plausible to identify this as a rare, and perhaps unusually complex loom. One possibility is that it was a low-warp loom with treadle-activated heddles developed from the table-form loom postulated for the horizontal one mentioned by Artemidorus. The dimensions given indicate that the second-hand loom was narrower than was required for the best quality one-piece tunics of the period. The usable width of Apollonia's loom would have been less than its estimated external width of 6 cubits. At least 1 cubit would have been required to accommodate the side supports and to allow space in which to insert and remove the shuttle. Support for the premise is given by the fact that the merchandise is identified simply as histos (ἱστός), by this date the common word for loom, not histos orthios (ἱστὸς ὄρθιος), the usual term for upright loom. Furthermore, its dimensions are given by width and length, not width and height, strong indication that it was not a high-warp loom.

Apollonia's loom was, then, unlikely to have been a simple rectangular timber frame such as is usual for high-warp looms. It could have been a treadle loom capable of weaving long, relatively narrow strips of cloth with such efficiency that Apollonia, and other Egyptian weavers with similar looms, were able to produce Tarsian-type linen more cheaply than the weavers of Tarsus itself, hence the lower prices for Alexandrian linen in chapters 26–28 of the Diocletian Edict. There is also the possibility that it may have been a loom for pattern weaving, even a prototype of the drawloom. Less than a century later fully developed drawloom textiles appear in Egypt. A number of these have survived including several fine, early ones now in the Textile Museum

(Trilling 1982:98–99, nos. 108–11). Number 108 is 1.29 m wide, Number 109 is 1.327 m, widths that could have been easily handled on Apollonia's loom with its external width of 2.70 m. In any case Apollonia must have seen the loom as a financial asset.

It is unlikely that changes in loom types happened very rapidly. The high-warp loom may have been retained for wide weaves such as those needed for tapestries, curtains, coverlets, and mantles, while the newer low-warp looms were used to produce woven lengths of cloth that could be stitched together to make whatever the buyer required in much less time than would be needed to weave the item to order. The Aezani segment of the Edict, the only one known that includes the part covering looms, chapter 12, lists four distinct types of loom, classified according to the material that was to be woven on them (Crawford and Reynolds 1977:135). One was for silk, one for part-silk, one for linen, and one for coarse utilitarian textiles. Only the top price that could be asked for the silk loom survives; it is 750 denarii. The value of the Aezani fragment lies in the indication it gives for the existence of a variety of looms in the early fourth century. In Egypt, judging from the evidence provided by changes in tunic construction, it appears that beginning in the fourth century, the high-warp loom was gradually replaced by possibly experimental versions of low-warp looms. At first this change may have had little effect on the construction of garments, but as the advantages of weaving narrower cloth became apparent, changes in tunic patterns were made. It can be estimated, then, that looms such as one represented in the thirteenth-century miniature in Cambridge, mentioned earlier, were the end result of at least eight hundred years development. Where the Coptic version of this low-warp loom is concerned, the major part of its development may have taken place between the late third century A.D., evidenced by the loom Apollonia bought in 298, and the narrower looms of the early seventh century whose remains were discovered at Epiphanius. For 1,000 years there are no significant depictions of floor looms, but the looms themselves changed during this time span— perhaps taking 800 years to complete their metamorphose.

# III. COPTIC TEXTILE DESIGN:
## *The Greek and Roman Sources*

OPTIC DESIGNERS created a distinctive textile style with a number of variants, most of them quickly recognizable. Coptic textiles are not easily confused with archaeological textiles found in other parts of the world. How such a variety of styles may have evolved is worthy of consideration even though positive conclusions cannot be reached for every instance.

It is notable that the configuration of the ornamentation of the textiles bears no resemblance to that of the few decorated textiles woven during the Dynastic period (Riefstahl 1944). What is even more unexpected, with almost no exceptions, the motifs decorating Coptic textiles do not derive from the well-established corpus of Egyptian ornament. Largely missing from Coptic textiles are the characteristic Egyptian lotus and papyrus motifs, for example, designs based upon feathers, and, perhaps most conspicuous by their absence, the many attractive symbols derived from Egyptian writing that were frequently used to decorate a wide range of objects during the Dynastic period. In addition, nothing in the style evolved by Coptic artists for human figures reflects the age-old conventions worked out early in the history of ancient Egypt and retained for centuries. Decorative motifs based upon the human form no longer conform to the strict ancient conventions that required heads and limbs to be depicted in profile and torsos in a near-frontal view.

The reasons for this abandonment of Egyptian decorative motifs and drawing conventions are not quickly apparent, and they must be sought in the social and historical background underlying the periods from which the Coptic textile style, with its several branches, was eventually born.

The character of Egyptian textiles had remained essentially unchanged for many centuries, as least so far as the textiles intended to be placed in burials were concerned. As closely as can be determined from the meager evidence available, marked changes in Egyptian weaving may have occurred only after the conquest of Egypt by Alexander the Great in the fourth century B.C. Patterned textiles made in Egypt before this date—the most important, perhaps, are the ones found buried with Tutankhamen—may have been isolated phenomena and not part of mainstream Egyptian weaving technology.

Alexander's conquest was relatively undisputed and, therefore, not particularly disruptive. The Egyptians had intensely disliked the Persians in control of Egypt at the time of the conquest and may not have given their rulers more than token support (Bell 1948). Persian religious beliefs and customs were totally foreign to the native Egyptians and were in some instances of a nature that the Egyptians found repellent. Alexander seems to have taken full advantage of this bias and was careful to make concessions to his new subjects.

Among other actions, he paid homage to the native gods. However, once accepted as king of Egypt, Alexander did not follow Egyptian customs to any significant extent, and he set in motion forces that were to alter some aspects of life in Egypt for centuries. When he founded Alexandria in the fall of 332 B.C., Alexander selected Dinocrates of Rhodes as his city's planner. Dinocrates laid out Alexandria as a model Greek city. Alexander's veterans who settled there lived and dressed as Greeks, as did their descendants for many generations. A few lived in other cities and villages throughout Egypt as well, but in these places, unlike Alexandria, they are believed to have been a minority, judging from the papyri (Turner 1968:82).

A$_{T FIRST}$, some of the textiles used by the Greeks and their associates may have been made by their women at home, following Greek and Macedonian custom from a remote period. Other textiles could have been made to their specifications by Egyptian servants and slaves. Specifications would have been necessary since Greek textiles of the period were unlike Egyptian ones in several respects, chiefly in material.

As described in section I, the textile technology that had been developed in Greece was based upon wool; flax was woven but rarely. Another fact is frequently missed by those familiar only with the depictions of textiles found in Classical and later Greek sculpture: some Greek textiles were elaborately patterned. Examples of garments made from textiles decorated with the figures of men and animals, plants, flowers, and geometric motifs can be found depicted in Greek art beginning in the late Geometric period and continuing

through the Hellenistic (Carroll 1965). There are even a few extant fragments of original decorated textiles. No examples belonging to the Ptolemaic period have been found in Egypt, but specimens of Hellenistic weaving dating from the fourth century B.C. to the early first century A.D. have been found in other regions, most notably in tombs in southern Russia and northern Mongolia (Stephani 1881:112–141, pl. 3–5; Trever 1932:29–33, pl. 1–3, 6–7). The material of these is wool, much of it dyed in rich, dark colors. The ornamentation was accomplished in a variety of ways: embroidery; tapestry; and a resist-dye technique, with figured, floral, and geometric motifs. The decoration of some specimens was executed in threads wrapped in strips of gold foil. In spite of their ragged and discolored condition, they are eloquent testimony to the rather extravagant taste of the Hellenistic period in the matter of textiles.

When Alexander died in 323 B.C., nearly 10 years after he had founded Alexandria, one of his most able generals, Ptolemy, son of Lagus, became the satrap of Egypt. This remarkable man was a writer as well as a soldier; he wrote an important memoir of his military experiences which is now largely lost, but was one of the sources used by Arrian for his history of Alexander (Bury 1958:175–176). Ptolemy was also a patron of poets and scholars. In 305 B.C., Ptolemy proclaimed himself king of Egypt and founded a dynasty that survived until 30 B.C. Almost from the beginning the Ptolemies demonstrated an ambivalent attitude toward their Egyptian subjects. Some of their actions were beneficial. Ptolemy continued, to some extent, the policy of cultural integration initiated by Alexander in the countries he had conquered. Among other matters, some historians think that, in Egypt, this involved the introduction of a deity, Serapis, who embodied attributes of both Greek and Egyptian gods. Supporting facts are obscure and open to dispute (Bell 1948:41). Ptolemy, an avid collector of books, together with his son established the *Museion* and its famous library. Around this time, too, additions were made to the Greek alphabet so Egyptian could be written as concisely as Greek. The beautiful but complex writing systems used earlier by the Egyptians did not encourage literacy, and reading and writing were largely left to specialists.

After the first two Ptolemies the actions taken by their successors ranged, for the greater part, from the insensitive to the repressive. None of the Ptolemies, as far as can be determined, went to the trouble of learning to speak the language of their subjects (Bell 1948). The last Ptolemaic queen, Cleopatra VII, may have been an exception: Plutarch describes her as a gifted linguist (Perrin 1920:196–197). Greek (actually Koine, an international form of Greek based upon Attic) was firmly established as the principal official language and remained so until the Arab conquest in the seventh century. Along with this linguistic bias the later Ptolemies were intolerant of nearly everything Egyptian, and went so far, in some periods and locations, as to forbid marriages between native Egyptians and Greeks (Bell 1948:42). The traditional forms of Egyptian art were held in particular disfavor. An unmistakable Greek stamp was placed upon all aspects of Egyptian culture. In 85 B.C. there was a native uprising, largely a reaction to heavy taxes and oppressive laws. This rebellion was put down with extreme severity, and an important Egyptian cult site, ancient Thebes, also known as the City of a Hundred Gates and the Eye of Ra, was destroyed.

It APPEARS LIKELY that the nearly total disappearance of Egyptian design motifs from major art forms and their replacement with others largely Classical in nature was caused by nearly three centuries of Greek rule with its accompanying repressions. However, the Ptolemaic rulers, even if they did not appreciate Egyptian sculpture and architecture may have recognized and valued the high degree of craftsmanship Egyptians brought to almost every branch of manufacture known at the time, including textile manufacture. Some changes in technology had to be made, Hellenistic taste in the matter of textiles being what it was as evidenced by the southern Russian and Mongolian textile finds. For example, military cloaks, an important article of male dress at this time, occasionally described in contemporary literature, were woven of wool; in the case of high-ranking officers, cloaks were likely to be red, purple, or dark blue, with the wearer's special insignia or other identifying designs done in tapestry weave or needlework. Demetrius Poliorcetes is said to have worn a riding cloak displaying the 12 signs of the zodiac; this garment was described by Athenaeus in his work, *The Deipnosophists*, book 12.535f (Gulick 1980:420–421). Figured textiles were hung as decoration during festivals, either on the walls of buildings or on the framework of large tents set up for the occasion. A remarkable example of this latter use was the banquet pavilion set up for his guests by Ptolemy Philadelphus, the first Ptolemy's son. Among other fine textiles decorating the pavilion were two sets of military cloaks hung as tapestries, one set woven with portraits of kings, the other with mythological scenes. This complex structure was described in a lost work of Callixeinus of Rhodes, the pertinent passages preserved by Athenaeus, book 5.196a–197c (Gulick 1967:387–393). A shrine in the palace of Ptolemy Philadelphus in Alexandria, decorated by his sister and queen, Arsinoë II, for an Adonis festival, was hung with richly patterned garments that were, according to one observer, fit for the gods (Gow 1950, no. 15). Many years later, Ptolemy's descendant, the famous Cleopatra, had a banquet tent hung with gold and purple-dyed textiles set up when she entertained Antony, this also according to Athenaeus, book 4.147e–f, quoting from another lost work (Gulick 1967:175). There are numerous examples that could be cited (Alexander 1978). The makers of all of these textiles may not have been Greek, but the fact that some of the design themes were Greek is significant.

ALONG WITH THIS taste for elaborately figured textiles, perhaps the very antithesis of Egyptian ideals, went an appreciation of well-made plain textiles. Still extant papyrus documents indicate that everyday wear for Greco-Egyptians was likely to be made from bleached or natural- color linen and wool cloth. An inventory of a man's wardrobe is among the "papers," of Zenon (Edgar 1925, no. 59092; Hunt and Edgar 1932:412–415) dating from 257 B.C. From this can be learned not only that summer garments were of linen and those for winter of wool, but also that a person with means could own what must have been an ample supply of garments.

Zenon had thirteen tunics, two of them with sleeves; nine outer wraps; and four pairs of socks. There is a possibility that these last may have been knitted. A number of examples of Coptic socks worked in a primitive type of knitting done with a single needle have been found (Burnham 1972), and the technique may have been known earlier. (The Coptic examples have a separate pocket for the big toe so they could be worn with thong sandals.) All of the textiles of Zenon's wardrobe could have been of Egyptian make.

Zenon was an agent or manager for Apollonius, the finance minister of the second Ptolemy whose banquet tent was mentioned previously. By a fortunate circumstance, an archive consisting of letters, memos, and other types of documents has survived and much of it has been published, the bulk of it by Edgar (1925, 1926, 1928). Zenon must have been a energetic man; he appears to have had a great many duties, a number of them connected with the raising of wool and the production of textiles. Some of his correspondence concerning wool production is cited in section I.

Egypt, as the first Ptolemy had reason to know by the time he elected to become its king, was a country whose population included many specially trained people. These were well accustomed to working in concert and under supervision, so a change from native Egyptian managers to Macedonian or Greek ones must not have created major difficulties so far as following rules and specifications was concerned. From a remote period, many Egyptian craftsmen, indeed much of the Egyptian population, had been accustomed to living and working conditions that were established for the benefit of the pharaohs and which were administered by the temples. A revealing example of this was discovered at the site of Deir el-

Medina, the home village of generations of workmen who constructed the tombs of the Valley of the Kings and the Valley of the Queens (Romer 1984). Both in the village and in the tombs were found documents of various types remarkable for the light they shed on the methods used by the Egyptians for planning and carrying out large and complex projects. Some Egyptians were clearly capable of preparing detailed plans for projects that might take years to complete. These plans included estimates of the supplies and manpower needed and set forth the order in which parts of the plan were to be carried out. Many ordinary people had learned to follow such plans and, at the same time, to live structured lives in circumstances that dictated not only aspects of their work but also of their personal lives, including, in some instances, what and how much they ate and drank. It is believed that villages similar to that discovered at Deir el Medina existed in other parts of Egypt as well, producing special goods or foodstuffs or carrying out large-scale building projects.

THE MACEDONIAN-GREEKS in Egypt took over and adapted some of the methods developed by the temples in the Dynastic period in order to ensure a continuous and profitable flow of goods and services. The papyri are evidence that the Macedonian-Greeks created a system of state controls, based in part upon the older system of controls developed by the temples in the Dynastic period, specifically for the textile industry (Bell 1948:49). Who could produce and sell textiles, what types of textiles could be sold, and how much could be charged for them were all subject to regulation. Part of these regulations concerned the materials and kinds of textiles that were woven; the type and extent of the ornamentation may have been covered as well.

UNDER THE PHARAOHS, the special skills developed by Egyptian artists and craftsmen had been devoted to serving the needs of the royal and priestly segments of the population. Under the Ptolemys, Egyptians produced instead luxury items for trade and for general consumption. Efforts were made to stimulate foreign trade. Egyptian craftsmen made glassware, writing papyrus, decorative alabaster objects, gold jewelry, and ivory carvings. They also prepared special materials, dyes, and pigments. These goods were sent all over the known world (Bell 1948:49). Luxury textile fibers—cotton, and perhaps silk—were imported from India (Johnson 1936:339), then woven into cloth, and exported along with the fine linen for which Egypt had long been famous. Other fancy textiles could have been made for export at this time as well: textiles similar, perhaps, to those mentioned previously, of the fourth century B.C. and later, which were found in Russian and Mongolian tombs. One of the southern Russian textiles, found covering a coffin in the sixth mound of the Seven Brothers, has figures on it with a Coptic look, rough in outline but filled with life, having been drawn in extremely active poses (Stephani 1881:120–130, pl. 4). The technique, a form of dyeing involving the use of a wax or gum resist, was later used by Coptic textile artists (Trilling 1982: 102–104).

The name of one early designer of figured textiles has been preserved— Pathymias (Gulick 1969:208–209). The Egyptian name suggests that the merging of Greek and Egyptian weaving traditions that later became an important feature of Coptic textiles had already started in the Ptolemaic period, and indicates that Egyptian weavers quickly adapted their art to suit Macedonian-Greek tastes. About this time, too, native Egyptian designs may have vanished from the general scheme of things, except for objects made for worshipers of Isis and Serapis. Even here, Greek taste tended to overwhelm the Egyptian subject matter; for example, the statuette of Harpocrates, found at Taxila, which depicts the infant Egyptian god as a plump Greek child with curling hair (Wheeler 1955:189). After all, now the goal was to please people who were not Egyptians.

For the Ptolemies, their subjects' weaving must have been a significant financial asset to be actively encouraged. The same was undoubtedly true for the Romans who took over Egypt after they defeated Cleopatra and Mark Antony in the battle of Actium in 31 B.C. Existing records provide a number of interesting details that show some of the ways the Macedonian-Greek, later Roman, bureaucracy affected textile making. Some examples: a papyrus stating the amount of weaving permitted a particular weaver (Grenfell, et al. 1900, no. 59), papyri relating to the sealing of looms in storage to prevent unauthorized use (Hunt and Smyly 1933, nos. 703, 769), ostraka weaving permits (Wilcken 1899, nos. 1154–1156; Preaux 1935, no. 75; Bagnall and Samuel 1976, nos. 143–144, 146–147). The collector of weaving fees was a special official assigned to oversee sales taxes (Grenfell and Hunt 1899, no. 736). There were also inspectors who checked all the business activities in their districts, including weaving shops (Hunt and Edgar 1934:34–39). The

system did several things, ensuring product quality while at the same time keeping the producers under close control by a series of tax assessments.

After the Roman conquest, Egypt became the personal property of Octavian, better-known as Augustus, and of all subsequent emperors. The majority of these emperors showed little interest in Egypt, except as a supplier of grain for the empire and as a source of revenue for maintaining the military forces of Rome. An exception was the grecophile Emperor Hadrian who founded Antinoöpolis in A.D. 130 during a visit to Egypt. Later this city became an important center for textile weaving, and many of the extant Coptic textiles were said by antiquities dealers to have been found there, including Numbers 17–26 of the Rietz Collection. A number of textiles claimed to derive from Antinoöpolis exhibit Greek design elements, the city-founder's interest in Greek art being considered sufficient reason for the attributions. However, there are other possible reasons for the classical design elements that appear in Coptic textiles, whether they in fact originate from Antinoöpolis or not. One possibility is the survival of Hellenistic elements; Egypt still retained a strong Greek element in its population after so many years of Ptolemaic rule. However, Hadrian was not the only Roman to be interested in Greek art—many were. Greek sculpture was collected to such an extent that little was left in Greece itself, and today many of the famous statues of antiquity are known only through Roman copies. Examples of other arts were prized too; Pliny, in books 33 and 34, tells of Romans who went to great lengths to acquire Greek silverplate and ornamental bronzes (Rackham 1968:112–113, 130–137).

This interest in Greek art has tended

to obscure the Roman contribution to Coptic textile design. The production of objects with Greek designs could have resulted from Roman commercial activities in Egypt. Roman overseers or their representatives may have encouraged or even mandated the use of Greek-derived motifs. While some Romans were able to collect original Greek art, others must have had to content themselves with copies. These could be quite elaborate, for example the famous *Alexander* mosaic, now in Naples, believed to be a copy of a major Greek painting. Some of the earliest textiles found in Egypt are fragments of what appear to be relatively large figured polychrome pieces woven in tapestry. Some are remarkable for being woven according to certain conventions for depicting the lights and shadows on objects in the real world; these are thought to have been developed by painters in the Hellenistic period. A frequently reproduced example is the *Fish Tapestry*, fragments of which are now at Lyons and Paris (Du Bourguet 1971:64, 76). It represents several different kinds of fish, realistically depicted, apparently swimming in shallow water. In style these polychrome textiles recall Hellenistic and Greco-Roman mural paintings such as are found on the walls of houses in Rome and Pompeii. Textiles with realistic designs such as the Lyons-Paris fish tapestry may be copies of paintings too, the result of a desire on the part of some to possess a replica of an original work of art that was also, in its own right, a tour de force.

Such textiles could represent a direct continuation of the Hellenistic-Ptolemaic tradition of figured textiles, perpetuated by the admiration for Greek antiquities. Eventually the techniques for weaving pictures may have become embodied in the regular training of weavers, right along with the techniques for weaving quantities of more ordinary types of cloth. From these roots could have come the development of the miniature tapestry panels used to decorate garments and domestic furnishings that are characteristic of certain varieties of Coptic textiles.

THE ROMAN OVERSEERS of the emperor refined the Ptolemaic tax collecting system and worked diligently to make certain that all able-bodied persons were active and productive so there would be taxes to collect. Individuals benefited from this policy only if they were large landholders or highly placed officials. Weaving, which had been essentially a cottage industry under the Ptolemies, became industrialized under the Romans. Romans who did not live on or own country estates set up to produce foodstuffs and domestic needs, including cloth, made increasing use of commercially produced textiles. Many of these must have been imported; as mentioned in section I, research has yielded little or no evidence for the existence of textile-producing guilds in major Roman cities (Frank 1940:201).

By the end of the third century, textiles were made in forty-three textile-manufacturing sites located throughout the known world, a number based upon Diocletian's Edict. There could have been more. Many of the Edict's parts pertaining to textiles are incomplete or missing. Even so, it is instructive to look at a map of the Roman Empire of this time with the place names of the Edict in mind—Barraclough has published one that is particularly useful in this respect (1979:88–89, map 1). Egypt, it is clear from the map, was but one supplier of textiles, though an important exporter of other valuable commodities as well (Barraclough 1979:91, map 2). Textile sources may have changed from one century to another, however. In literature and in the business papyri there are other textiles identified by geographical names not listed in the Edict. Various records, summarized by Forbes (1956:232–235), indicate that textiles from many places, distant and relatively near, were sold in the markets of Rome, including the textiles of Egypt, also mentioned in the Edict.

Egyptian linen had long been highly regarded for its quality and was regularly exported. In addition, by the Roman period, Egyptian weavers, working with wool from the improved breeds of sheep developed under the Ptolemies, had certainly learned to weave textiles from this material. They may also have learned to imitate specialty textiles similar to or identical with those made in other places. If they did not do this immediately, they must have done it eventually, as witness the Tarsian-type textiles woven in or exported from Alexandria. As stated in the introduction, this commercial practice, making types of goods that copied or imitated particular items first made elsewhere, was not unusual—at least not by A.D. 301, the time of the edict which records some of them. The practice may have been carried on for no other reason than to provide a popular item that was either in short supply or too highly priced for many consumers. Furthermore, some of the merchandise, the Tarsian linen from Alexandria in particular, may not have been less good than the textiles copied, only less costly.

Papyrus records that mention textiles often identify them by names derived from countries. There are, for example,

textiles designated Spanish and Italic (Grenfell et al. 1907, no. 405; Meyer 1911, no. 10). Precisely what characterized these different weaves has not been preserved. Equally mysterious are their origins. Were they textiles from Spain and Italy? Or were they textiles copied from others made in these countries? Or—a not too remote possibility—were they textiles of Coptic design, but specifically made for export in styles, colors, and qualities known to be pleasing to the residents of these countries? This last has been proposed by Johnson, who points out papyrus records that indicate that special textiles were made for trade in the East (1936:338). Certain types of textiles identified by foreign place names are thought to have been woven in Egypt. One, described as being striped, was termed Laconian, that is, Spartan (Hunt and Edgar 1932:334–337; Grenfell et al. 1907, no. 406).

THE VARIOUS WEAVING towns of Egypt are thought to have specialized, producing textiles woven in distinctive designs and colors; this notion helps to explain the visual variety of the extant Coptic textiles. The custom may have started in the Ptolemaic period, when the town of Tanis was evidently known as a place that produced desirable bedcovers not available elsewhere (Edgar 1925, no. 59048). Various references to specialty textiles made in specific places occur, though rarely with any descriptions of the appearance of the textiles. One town with a distinctive design style may have been Arsinoë (Petrie 1909, no. 208). Records indicate that a number of other weaving towns may have had individual styles also (Johnson 1936:338). Two famous weaving towns were Thebes and Oxyrhynchus. Textile varieties possibly named after geographical regions, Cynopolite, Sinaru, and Xoitic, are cited by Forbes (1956:237).

The weavers of Alexandria and its environs were famous for producing textiles in a style named polymita, or so Pliny would have us believe (Rackham 1967:136–137). These were typified by the use of yarns dyed in bright, clear colors (Ker 1919:492–493). The Alexandrine textile style seems, from its description, to have been a continuation of the *poikilos* (ποικίλος) textile style of Greece, at least in a general way. Polychrome textiles are frequently mentioned in literature. The earliest citations occur in the Homeric epics, where Athena receives a *poikilos* dress in the Iliad (6:294–297), (Monro and Allen 1954). An identical dress is given to Telemachus (for his future bride) by Helen in the Odyssey (15:107–108), (Allen 1951). The multicolor Coptic textiles could well derive from this tradition. With the Alexandrine textiles, though, a new element has entered, the weaving of patterns by skipping over groups of threads, either warp or weft ones, in a regular sequence so as to form a pattern. It is of interest to note, in this connection, that one piece in the Rietz Collection, Number 88, was woven on a dyed linen warp composed of threads of three different colors, regularly arranged, the sequence being blue, yellow, and brown. None of this can be seen in the tapestry portion that is all that remains, but the ground must have been woven in a way that took advantage of the colored warps. A twill is a possibility. It is tempting to identify this fragment as an example of Alexandrian polymita.

At some point after Egypt became a province of Rome, dress standards changed and became Roman instead of Greek or Egyptian. The details of the change are unclear and may actually have been rather minor. Tradition has it that the principal garment, the dalmatic, worn by both men and women, was introduced by Emperor Elagabulus early in the third century. This garment, a long-sleeved, straight- sided tunic, is not too unlike a garment sometimes worn by Hellenistic Greeks and may have, therefore, existed in Egypt earlier. Two of Zenon's tunics are described as having sleeves, suggesting that they might have been a form of dalmatic. What little has survived of the garments and other textiles used during the early centuries of Roman rule in Egypt is not particularly informative on this point. The portraits painted in encaustic that were part of the burial practices of the time sometimes show a part of the garment worn. In the case of male portraits, the garment can generally be identified as a white tunic decorated with plain purple shoulder bands. Half-length portraits in cartonnage may also include a representation of an outer garment trimmed with a decorated square or roundel. Outside Egypt, representations of similar garments in paintings and mosaics show that the sleeves were ornamented too, but with narrower bands, often doubled.

R EFERENCES in ancient literature (summarized by Wilson 1938) provide information that can be applied to the problem. In early Roman times the wearing of purple bands, called *clavi*, was limited to particular classes of Roman citizens. The width of the bands was regulated by law according to the rank of the wearer. The wearing of entirely purple garments was limited to the emperor and, under certain special conditions, important generals. It is not certain how strictly this limitation of the use of the color purple was followed in later times, particularly in Egypt during the Roman period. Custom, rather than law, may have become the arbiter. It must be understood, though, that Egyptians in the early centuries of the present era lived with the burden of a rigid class system. Egyptians with the necessary documentation and money for fees often tried to improve their status a degree or two by legal means. An important group of papyri concerns the upgrading of social status by the process of application and examination (Nelson 1979).

In societies with well-defined social grades it is common for the different classes to dress so as to make their status visually, thus immediately, identifiable. The distinguishing marks take many forms, but in the case of the Copts, Roman custom with regard to the use of purple may have been adopted. Many of the surviving Coptic garment ornaments are worked in purple- dyed wool and consist in large part of plain or simply decorated bands and rectangles. Such pieces might have indicated the social position of the wearer, at least in the opening decades of the present era, perhaps later.

The bands and stripes that commonly decorate Coptic tunics are, possibly, Roman in derivation. Even less certain is the origin of the decorated squares, circles, and ovals that are an equally common feature of Coptic tunic ornamentation. The themes often derive from Greek mythology, but the Romans found this subject matter of interest as well, though perhaps for different reasons. Here, however, the two streams come together to create the distinctive Coptic textile style. On tunics, the ornaments were often

positioned to lie above the shoulders and in front of the knees of the wearer, vulnerable points, it should be noted, susceptible to disease and crippling injuries. This fact suggests that the positioning of these ornaments originated in a widespread belief that glances from the eyes of certain people could cause harm, in some instances, even without the owner of the "evil eye" being aware of it.

Both Greeks and Romans believed in the evil eye, and the Egyptians may have done so too, though this is less certain. Elworthy, in his introduction to his study on the subject, collects references to the evil eye belief from ancient literature, Greek and Latin as well as the Bible. The importance of such a belief, how it affected daily life and the mindset of those who held it is not too apparent from these writings. All too often the writers themselves do not seem to have been believers and are therefore unconvincing. Yet the notion persists, and studies in the field done not long ago show that in modern rural Greece, not only does belief in the evil eye persist, it persists in a form that the investigators theorize has survived for several thousands of years (Blum and Blum 1970:309–310).

Defenses against the evil eye are of several classes. One is a design incorporated into something worn, a design that has the form of an eye, or eyes, that by staring back counteracts the evil gaze (Elworthy 1970:126–142). Another is a design of such fascination or complexity that it traps the gaze, as it were, preventing it from working diabolical harm (Cirlot 1962:165–167. A third defense is a gesture of a mildly threatening nature, perhaps an upraised hand, sometimes with the fingers held in particular ways (Elworthy 1970:243–254). It is interesting to note that all three of these devices commonly appear in Coptic textile decoration. The eyes of the figures decorating textiles are often quite pronounced, especially those of warriors, for example Rietz Numbers 20, 24, and 27, perhaps contributing to the wearer's protection. A beautiful interlace, a favorite devil-trap motif, that would certainly engage the attention of anyone's eye can be seen on Rietz Number 4. Figures with raised hands are particularly common, Rietz Numbers 16, 24, 25, 31, 32, and 33. Of course, many other interpretations are possible—some will be discussed further on. Moreover, different people may have understood the same symbols in ways that suited their own personal beliefs.

The OVERALL STYLE of Coptic textiles evolved, then, from both Greek and Roman elements. There was the introduction into Egypt of a taste for colored, decorated textiles such as had long been a tradition in Greek culture, with, at the same time, the suppression of traditional Egyptian design motifs, except for a few symbols related to the worship of Isis and Serapis. Later, Roman customs regarding the use of purple bands on garments became widespread as the Roman Empire expanded, reaching Egypt at a time not known precisely. Roman taste may have encouraged the revival or continuation of Greek motifs, and possibly of other types of motifs as well, even some Egyptian ones. However, from the third century, and possibly earlier, the designs favored by weavers for the bands and roundels or squares were derived for the greater part from Greek and Roman sources. Elaborate geometric patterns of varieties found in floor mosaics throughout the Roman Empire commonly occur in the ornamentation of Coptic garments. Equally common are motifs matching the floral themes favored by Hellenistic Greek artists, often combined with figures, human and animal, in poses that illustrate Greek myths. Uniting the figured and the geometric motifs are their orderly placement on garments: shoulder bands, double sleeve bands, and round or rectangular panels set in the areas of the shoulders and knees. Reasons for this placement cannot be determined with certainty; belief in the evil eye, as suggested above, is but one possibility. Another reason could be the preservation of health or the alleviation of some chronic illness such as arthritis. In a related vein, tying one's belt cord in a square knot was thought to safeguard health, a practice recorded by Pliny, book 28.17.64 (Jones 1975:46, 47). This particular knot, once known as the knot of Hercules, was believed in antiquity to have therapeutic qualities over and above its more familiar use as a bandage or surgical knot. This may explain its appearance, in stylized form, on such Coptic textiles as Rietz Number 17.

The occurrence in the corpus of Coptic textiles of so many variant forms of textiles may be explained by the presumed commercial aspects of much Coptic weaving, aimed either at copying other textiles or developing attractive original styles that would appeal to buyers. Added to this may have been religious or philosophical aspects that influenced the selection and development of certain motifs. These will be considered next.

# IV. COPTIC MOTIFS:
## *Some Philosophical Concepts*

MAJOR PART of the interest roused by Coptic textiles derives from the subject matter found in their decoration. Some of the more elaborate ornaments contain groups of figures that can be identified as participants in familiar myths and legends. Two particularly elaborate examples, one a hanging depicting a queen or goddess, the other a hanging with the story of Attis, have been analyzed by Friedlander (1945) and show how complex the symbolism used by Coptic textile designers could be. Often, though, one or two figures sufficed to indicate a myth or myth cycle. The significance of these is sometimes not at all obvious, and the actual meaning of a particular motif may have depended upon the views, beliefs, or superstitions of the wearer.

The motifs that ornament Coptic textiles are varied in themselves but can be divided into two principal groups—textiles with motifs drawn from subjects that are animate or inanimate, and textiles with symmetrical geometric motifs constructed from straight or curved lines. Of examples in the second, non-representative group, the most striking are squares, roundels, and bands enclosing elaborate geometric interlaces—woven labyrinths as it were. The motifs are worked in monochrome, generally purple or dark blue, on a ground of undyed yarn. The textiles of the first group fall naturally into two subgroups. The first is monochrome. The second subgroup is polychrome

and tends to be less formal in concept. The motifs themselves are based upon vegetation, vines, leaves, flowers, and fruit; artifacts, vases, baskets, and parts of buildings; assorted birds, fish, and beasts, both real and mythical; and human and superhuman beings. The human figures are represented, for the most part, as warriors, dancers, hunters, horsemen, and charioteers, and some of them have attributes that identify them as particular legendary persons. Among the nonhuman beings are centaurs, mermaids, satyrs, and winged figures, usually erotes, as well as richly dressed human-shaped figures that can be identified as gods and goddesses of the ancient Classical pantheon. Though most are miniature in scale, the figures convey a strong sense of vitality, being shown in active poses, often with greatly emphasized eyes that add to the impression of liveliness. All of these subjects, the real and the imagined, are drawn with varying degrees of finesse; some are crude to the point of being barely recognizable. Nearly all convey the impression of being protagonists in an ongoing story. Fruit and floral garlands are combined with some of the figured motifs, often worked in improbable colors as are the strange trees and plants that may fill spaces not occupied by figures.

At the beginning of this study, believing, as many historians have done, that the wearers of Coptic textiles were primarily Christian in belief, I attempted to locate Christian themes among Coptic decorative motifs. Surprisingly there are few obviously Christian themes to be found. Most are late and derived from stories in the Old Testament. Christian themes in the corpus of Coptic textiles when viewed in its entirety are vastly outnumbered by those that appear to have absolutely no connection with early Christian symbolism. It might be claimed that the persecution of Christians discouraged them from openly displaying the symbols of their religion, and that many of the apparently pagan symbols actually had hidden meanings that related to Christianity. But exactly what Christian truth can be hidden in the story of Pasiphaë and the bull, for example, or the story of the death of Attis, both themes found on Coptic textiles? It is a fact, too, that the bulk of the extant textiles were woven after Constantine made Christianity the state religion, when Christians were perfectly free to express their beliefs as they saw fit, even to wear the motifs of their religion woven into their dress. Pagans, not Christians, were those likely to persecuted. So the question arises, why do pagan themes outnumber Christian ones?

IN SEEKING an answer to the foregoing question it is important to understand that the first millennium of the present era was a time of varied beliefs and philosophies, among which Christianity was but one of several (Bell 1975). Throughout the Roman Empire this period saw the development and growth of many different religious and philosophical beliefs.

In Egypt, as well as in other parts of the Roman Empire, Christianity came into direct competition with beliefs descended from the mystery religions of late antiquity. One of the most prominent of these was centered around Isis, a goddess native to Egypt. Related belief systems held by Egyptians as well as by others in the Roman Empire were based upon the mythic lives of gods originally Greek—Dionysus, Orpheus, and Helios. This may explain the presence of Greek themes in the repertory of Coptic textile designs, especially figures derived from Greek myth. Two examples in the Rietz Collection, both rather late, are Numbers 42 and 55, representing, respectively, Orpheus with his lyre and Dionysus with his followers: nymphs and satyrs. One important cult had as its principal figure the Persian god Mithras. Motifs of the kinds employed by Persian designers are fairly common in Coptic textiles, the so-called Tree-of-life, represented in the collection by Number 36, was a special favorite, but any connection with Mithras is entirely conjectural.

Philosophies derived from Roman and Greek thinkers were associated with some of these religions or were followed as tenets for living, apart from a religious creed: Stoicism, Neoplatonism, or the nearly related Neopythagoreanism. This last embodied certain esoteric beliefs about numbers and geometric figures based upon combinations of numbers, and it is tempting to see a connection between this philosophy and the geometric designs found on certain Coptic textiles, for example, Rietz Number 8.

Judaism was very much alive in Egypt at this period too, though in a state of philosophical flux, and some Jews in Alexandria read the Old Testament in a Greek translation made for their benefit. The sacrifice of Isaac, a popular Coptic textile motif, is represented in the Rietz Collection by Number 56, in a late example made nearly indecipherable by repeated, careless copying.

In addition to these there were religious systems newly formulated by individuals who lived and taught in the first centuries of the present era. Egyptian Gnosticism (in its Valentinian form) and Manichaeanism, like Christianity, were the contributions of historical men whose lives and words are known from contemporary and near-contemporary records. Dualism, an attempt to explain good and evil, makes an appearance in both Gnosticism and Manichaeanism, and certain Coptic textile designs seem to be attempting to convey the principle; an interesting example is Rietz Number 33.

By following one or the other of these religions or religious philosophies, an individual living in Egypt could add rich, colorful dimensions to what, at best, must have been a hard, dull, and hopeless life. It was rarely possible to better one's social status, once established by birth. A papyrus document of the second century A.D. illustrates the complexities of the laws governing marriages between people of different ethnic origins or social classes and also the strict regulations concerning inheritances. Most infractions led to the confiscation of the money and property in question (Johnson 1936:711–717). This document vividly illustrates the existence of discrimination based upon ethnic origin, former slave status, sex, and age. Unwanted children were exposed upon trash heaps, and anyone compassionate enough to rescue and raise them as their own could suffer severe penalties. Poor people of low social status could not even hope to improve their own lot by marriage or the lot of their children by giving them up for adoption. Those with money for fees were allowed to petition to raise

their social status, and many did (Nelson 1979), but there is no way of knowing how often petitions were successful and how often they, too, landed on the local trash heap.

I N ATTEMPTING to identify any possible meanings the motifs of Coptic textiles may have had for those who chose to display them on their garments and decorative woven items, it is necessary to take into account philosophical and religious beliefs that were part of the social climate of the times and which often resulted in what would now be called civil disobedience, severe clashes between citizens of opposing beliefs (Jones 1963). Judging from the amount of blood that was shed and the human misery that resulted, the people who lived during the first millennium took their beliefs seriously indeed.

What follows is not intended to be a complete exposition of then current religious and philosophical systems. It is merely an outline sketch that suggests the numbers and natures of the beliefs prevalent at the time Coptic textiles were evolving their characteristic forms. More complete information on the subject of first-millennium belief systems can be found in Dodds (1965), Atiya (1968), Bell (1975), and Pagels (1981).

In the opening centuries of the present era, Egyptians held beliefs that ranged from the highly cerebral to the simple. Alexandria was still a center of intellectual activity that attracted scholars from other regions; among them were Philo, a Jewish apologist philosopher, and, later, an even more famous learned Jew, John Mark, known to history as Saint Mark the Evangelist. These and others of like interests taught and wrote and attracted personal followings, often sizeable in number. People of less intellectual bent occupied their thoughts with a variety of religious beliefs and superstitions. At the lowest level, the credulous made use of rituals—often involving preparations of revolting-sounding substances—and invocations, intended, for the greater part, to improve their chances in love, increase income, and foresee the future. The literate among them could make use of handbooks containing directions for various types of magical activities. One of these, known as the Leiden Papyrus, has survived, and was recently collated by Betz (1986). It was written in the first half of the third century in Egyptian, in the demotic script, but with many glosses in Greek, an indication of the bilingual nature of Egyptian life at the time (Griffith and Thompson 1974). At whatever level, personal beliefs must have helped many to endure a difficult period in history.

It is thought that the circumstances of contemporary life contributed to the emphasis some Egyptians placed upon intellectual and spiritual matters. Under Roman rule Egyptian culture became fixed, even stagnant. People who were not slaves but who were unable to break out of their low social class often left Roman-held countries entirely, or else sank to the level of serfs on large estates. By the time of the arrival of the Holy Family, soon after the birth of Christ, everyday life in Egypt was monotonous and lacked any stimulus other than that of satisfying the unceasing demands of the Roman overseers. The dullness and hopelessness of real life tended to encourage the revival of the ancient Egyptian belief in an afterlife of superior quality and spiritual development.

Since its inception in Ptolemaic times,

the official religion in Egypt had centered around Serapis. Serapis worship was limited almost exclusively to Memphis and Alexandria in Egypt, but the cult of Serapis and his consort Isis, an important Egyptian goddess of great antiquity, spread throughout the Roman Empire and had many followers, the Emperor Domitian among them. Depictions of the two deities are common in the art of the first and of succeeding centuries; even textile portraits of these gods were sometimes made. There is a small woven portrait of Isis in the Rietz collection, originally a garment decoration (Rietz Number 39). However, not everyone found the Isis-Serapis cult suited to their personal emotional needs. The more intellectually inclined developed an interest in Greek or Roman philosophical concepts. Stoicism, not surprisingly, was favored as a philosophy although there was also a revival of the ancient Greek philosophy of Pythagoras.

The cult of Mithras, with its promise of redemption after death, had a strong hold on many. It was essentially a religion for free males, particularly soldiers, which excluded many from the comforts of its beliefs. When John Mark arrived in Alexandria some years after the middle of the first century with a message about a similar, but more inclusive, religion, many people were ready to listen to him.

Some Egyptians must have found John Mark's message inspiring, because when he made his second visit to Alexandria he discovered that he had a significant number of followers. Others, in particular the worshipers of Serapis, were disturbed by John Mark's message and also by the growing size of his congregation. The success of the Evangelist in attracting converts aroused the ire of the priests of the established religion, and they, in turn, raised the anxiety of their followers as to the ultimate intentions of the Christians. Coptic tradition has it that matters between the two factions came to a boil on Easter, A.D. 68, which that year coincided with the festival of Serapis (Atiya 1968:27). Rumors that the images of the gods were in danger of being destroyed by the Christians were spread. In response, a mob of Serapis worshippers attacked the Christian congregation, put a rope around John Mark's neck, and dragged him to his death. This violent incident, if indeed it took place, must have alerted the Roman authorities to the fact that the Christians were potential troublemakers, but it seems to have had little effect on official Roman policy toward Christians.

For over a century after the introduction of Christianity, believers lived quietly and avoided attracting attention to themselves. A few attained positions of trust, and some even amassed property. Then, near the end of the second century, the state-sponsored persecution of all religious dissidents began. Restrictions were placed upon many, perhaps the most severe upon Christians. Even so, increasing numbers of people became Christian converts in spite of the inconveniences and, often, danger. In all likelihood these converts found Christian tenets comforting and strengthening in a period that, overall, had very little to offer in the way of personal safety or material benefits.

This growth in Christian membership made the authorities increasingly uneasy. In A.D. 202 an edict was issued by the Emperor Septimius Severus that was specifically intended to halt conversions. From this date onwards there were periods of persecution alternating with periods of tolerance until 284, the start of the reign of Diocletian, promulgator of the famous Edict. His rule marks the beginning of the Era of Martyrs during which massive, systematic persecutions took place. The year of his accession is Year One in the Coptic Christian calendar; the exact day, September 11th, is the Coptic New Year's Day.

From a modern viewpoint, the decision to persecute certain groups of people was a move born of desperation, one that deprived the Roman Empire of many of its most able people. It must be remembered that while Christians were not the only targets, as events transpired they were the principal sufferers. At the bottom of the Roman decision to persecute was the fact that important civil and military positions were held by educated, literate people, many of them believers in the Christian faith. The philosophical foundations of early Christianity may have made it attractive to those already well-read in Greek philosophy and perhaps familiar with certain of the more esoteric tenets of ancient Egyptian religion. For years Roman authorities had had no objection to any particular religion as a belief system, even when held by individuals charged with important administrative responsibilities. In this they were more tolerant than many rulers of more recent date. Most of the extant popular religions were similar anyway, in that they espoused some form of belief in an afterlife and were essentially monotheistic. Christianity, though, carried the latter belief to a level that made it impossible for its serious adherents to acknowledge the Roman emperor as a deity, even by performing the symbolic act of burning incense before a statue of the current emperor in lieu of the more involved sacrifice usually offered (Hunt and Edgar 1934:352–355).

The sadism with which those who refused to burn incense before a statue were put to death can only be understood as a clear indication of how serious the Romans considered the situation to be. Estimates of the number of people who were executed during a period of about 10 years varies from 144,000 to 800,000; in any case numerous enough to create an ominous, terror-filled environment for the survivors. Yet the numbers of Christians continued to grow.

In 313, the Edict of Milan put an end to the persecution of Christians and also restored confiscated property. This edict was promulgated by Constantine, in what looks like an astute political move against his arch-rival, Valerius Licinianus Licinius, whose policy was firmly anti-Christian, as were his followers. At first Constantine proclaimed general religious toleration, but when he became sole emperor, and had possibly taken time to assess conditions, he established Christianity as the state religion. He also showed a degree of intolerance for certain pagan practices; though he himself was technically pagan for most of his life. His reasons for not being baptised until he was near death are still debated (Jones 1964:81).

One of the pagan practices affected by the establishment of Christianity was mummification. This ancient Egyptian custom had survived both the Greek and the Roman conquest, but had been falling into disuse for reasons both social and economic. Now, early in the fourth century, it was abandoned entirely. A consequence of this change in burial practice was the preservation of textiles that had been woven for the use of the living rather than for burial

with the dead as had been the case previously. Instead of the involved, decorative bandaging of the corpse with long strips of plain-weave linen, the dead were now dressed in the garments they had worn in life and laid on a board, a pillow under the head. Surviving specimens of burial textiles often have mends and patches, indication that they had been used before burial and were not new. Large textiles such as shawls, bed coverlets, curtains— whatever could be spared, possibly— were used for the external wrappings. The whole bundle was then laid directly in the ground. Where the soil conditions were right, preservation of both body and garments was assured, and from this point onward the history of Coptic textiles can be illustrated by real textiles, not depictions in art or descriptions in literature.

After the death of Constantine in 337, there was a period of conflict as various sons and other relatives strove to succeed him. Victory was ultimately won in 361 by Julian, known to history as the Apostate (Browning 1976). Like Constantine before he became a Christian, Julian worshiped Helios, the sun god, but also supported other non-Christian religions. He tried to organize a pagan church around the old gods, but gave it a monotheistic emphasis. He appears to have been supported by members of the old aristocracy who had retained philosophical and religious beliefs established in Classical antiquity. One of these, Orphism, related to Pythagoreanism, was either revived or came out of hiding. The chief deity was Dionysus, an ancient Greek god who appears rather frequently in Coptic textiles (Lenzen 1960). Orphism was a mystic, religious sect that among other gentle practices made offerings of incense while reciting poems dedicated to a variety of gods and spirits. In contrast, Julian himself liked presiding over bloody public sacrifices of large numbers of animals. He did, though, extend special favors to all worshipers of the old gods, and there is evidence that his influence was felt even in places as remote from the center of the empire as the British Isles. What has been identified as a fourth-century A.D. Orphic temple was recently discovered in England (Walters 1982). The elaborate floor mosaics of this building include depictions of sea creatures that in style and subject matter resemble certain Coptic textiles of this period and later.

Julian's reign lasted only two years, but it both alarmed and angered Christian leaders. The pagan resurgence his reign inspired lasted for half a century. Details not retained by written history about this period can be found in art. The fact that there was a resurgence, or at least a coming out of hiding, is suggested by the predominance of pagan themes depicted in Coptic textile ornaments of the late fourth century. The finest of these are in monochrome and combine geometric interlaces with panels containing figures from Classical myths. Ivy and vine-leaf motifs, both connected with the worship of Dionysus and his follower, Orpheus, are extremely common on textiles of the period and may reflect pagan beliefs.

There were violent aftermaths to Julian's reign. Julian, evidently, had found sympathizers among those who had not willingly espoused Christianity under Constantine. Some of these holdouts were members of the established aristocracy. These unfortunates and their families became the prime targets of militant monks who set out to intimidate worshipers of Serapis and to wipe all non-Christian religions from the face of the earth. In many bloody confrontations, temples were destroyed by mobs that were incited and led by Christian monks. In 411, a mob led by no less a person than Patriarch Theophilus himself stormed and destroyed the principal Serapis temple at Alexandria and, at the same time, the major part of the great Ptolemaic library of the *Museion*. Of this library, little was left for the Arabs to burn in the seventh century, if in fact they actually did. In some circles this story is thought to be an invention of later historians (Aitya 1968:81). As a final atrocity, in 415, a little more than a century after Constantine's first proclamation of general religious toleration, Hypatia, a neoplatonist philosopher, a mathematician, and one of the foremost women of her time, was stoned to death by a Christian mob. She had had students, friends, and admirers of all philosophical persuasions; her cruel death marked the end of open associations between scholars of unlike beliefs for years to come.

T HE WAY WAS now clear for Christian leaders to turn their attention to internal problems of a theological nature. Earlier, certain Christian scholars had united in attacking the Gnostics. Two second-century Alexandrine teachers, Valentinus and Basilides, developed this highly esoteric cult, based upon pre-Christian and pagan antecedents. It was deliberately mysterious in character, in part a protective device against informal persecution, and may have included some magical practices. It had unusual features for the time: women were allowed near-equality with men in religious exercises, and the supreme deity seems to have been female (Pagels 1981:57–83). More orthodox Christians found these features objectionable. Even worse, Gnostics rejected martyrdom instead of welcoming it as a chance to demonstrate their faith. Gnostics themselves did not consider martyrdom particularly meritorious and avoided it whenever possible.

Secretive from the beginning, Gnostic believers are thought to have eventually "gone underground" to survive, some of them gradually absorbing the Manichaean doctrine of the dual godhead. The founder of Manichaenism, a Persian named Mani, was a historical person who had been put to death in A.D. 273 by Varahran I. According to tradition, Mani had suffered crucifixion. He had followers in Egypt as late as the caliphate of al-Mahdi in the eighth century, and some of them may have been in fact Gnostics. If so, this may explain some of the mysterious-appearing designs on Coptic textiles of the late period.

As late as the early 1940s almost all that could be learned about Gnosticism was derived from historical accounts written by contemporary or near contemporary opponents, who were biased at best. In the fourth century, when the serious persecutions of Christians by fellow Christians began, one or more members of the Gnostic sect gathered together a large group of proscribed writings and hid them. In 1945 these were found, packed in a terracotta jar buried in a cave not far from the ancient monastery of Saint Pachomius. The books may have been part of the library there (for the story of their discovery see Pagels 1979:xi–xvi). The books were largely Coptic translations of Greek texts, verse and prose, often incorporating a rich and varied symbolism with origins both pagan and canonical Christian. These have recently been made available in an English translation (Robinson 1981), so it is now possible to speculate, at least, upon the possibly Gnostic origins of some Coptic textile motifs.

OTHER CHRISTIAN sects were more aggressive than the Gnostics, and stayed in the open to join battle, a conflict sometimes verbal, with formally expressed curses hurled back and forth, sometimes involving actual bloodshed. The disagreements were caused by doctrinal differences. Matters came to a head during the Fourth Ecumenical Council at Chalcedon which condemned the Monophysite doctrine of the Copts, which held that Jesus Christ was one person from two persons, God and man, and had one nature. Instead it was claimed that Jesus Christ was one person with two natures. The real issue was a political power struggle, and the See of Alexandria, long the dominant leader in Christian affairs, lost. The Coptic church became permanently separated from the rest of Christianity which Coptic Christians branded as diophysite. Each side denied the charges of the opposite side and held firm to their own interpretation. The result of the disagreement was to split the Coptic church—that is, the Egyptian church—from the rest of Christendom and to create a number of conflicting doctrines that caused trouble for generations. The issues that define the beliefs of Monophysite, Monothelite, and Melkite Christians are complex and need not be further clarified here. Interested persons are referred to Atiya (1968:69–78) who also details the historical consequences. It appears unlikely that these particular arguments generated textile designs to illustrate their complexities.

What is important is that divisions were created between Christian and Christian, between close relatives, even between the Melkite Emperor Justinian and his consort, Empress Theodora. She secretly favored Monophysitism and protected its adherents whenever possible. In Egypt, persecutions of Monophysites as severe as any promulgated by the pagan emperors against Christians occurred, directed by the Byzantine-appointed patriarchs of Alexandria. The patriarchs were ordered to convert the Copts to the version of Christianity favored by Byzantine rulers. They went about their task with utmost brutality: the bloodiest of these was the Patriarch Cyrus. After 10 years of Cyrus's activities, not only was Byzantine rule highly unpopular, everything associated with this rule—language, literature, and even the official style of art—was thoroughly detested. This hatred, as much as anything else, may explain the perceived "degeneration" of human figures depicted in late Coptic art. When Egypt was attacked by the Arabs, the native Egyptians did virtually nothing to assist Cyrus to defend their country, and Egypt came under Muslim rule (Atiya 1968:78).

THE ARAB conquerors of Egypt rarely troubled to differentiate between the different varieties of Christian believers among their new subjects. This gave those Copts who had been persecuted for their Monophysite beliefs respite, and they made good use of it, as mentioned in the Introduction. The complexities of the situation, the advantages and disadvantages experienced by the Copts after the Arab conquest, have been described by Atiya (1986:79–98).

The immediate effect was a revival of Coptic art and literature. The style of drawing used for human and animal figures decorating textiles changed markedly. Gone were the formal poses and the dark, subdued color schemes favored by Byzantium. Instead, the drawing of figures became increasingly abstract until a point was reached when figures, animal or human, were nearly or completely unrecognizable. A notable example in the Rietz Collection is a fragmentary tunic, Number 65. A single textile might be ornamented with five, six, or more bright colors, along with black and white. The favorite background color was red, either rosy or orange-tinged. This change is thought by some to signify degeneration, but it is better understood as a shift in taste.

There is also an underlying current of iconoclasm which came to a head in Byzantium in the eighth century. This may have affected Coptic designers. Muslim attitudes toward representations of living things could have had an effect as well, though prohibitions against depictions of humans and animals were less fixed in the early years of the Islamic faith than they became later.

Many Copts possessed skills that their Arabian rulers did not, mainly literacy and familiarity with the systems required for administering a densely populated country like Egypt with a tradition of close bureaucratic control. Arabia was a far different country at this time, and such organization as existed was based upon family and tribal relationships. Knowledgeable Copts lost no time in making themselves useful. The situation for the Copts became less favorable later, when they were heavily taxed and at times were denied privileges such as the right to ride horses. Often Copts were forced to wear special clothing or accessories that identified them as Christians. In some periods this meant garments with a yellow or orange ground, a feature commonly seen in later textiles.

Even with these problems, some individuals evidently led useful, productive lives and even made cultural and technical contributions. It was a Coptic Christian architect who, in the ninth century, designed and built the pointed arch nearly two centuries before the discovery of this useful structural feature by European architects (Atiya 1968:86). Craftsmen in other media flourished and helped advance their respective fields. Much of what is most refined in Islamic craftsmanship of later periods is rooted in Coptic technology (Du Bourguet 1971:158). But with the passing of time, Coptic textiles became increasingly more Arabic in design, and it is difficult to decide upon a terminal date for the long series of Coptic textiles. The tenth, eleventh, and twelfth centuries are all possibilities.

In the eleventh century the early Crusades brought new troubles to the Copts. As Monophysites, they were viewed by Europeans as heretics. At the same time the Arabs saw them as Christians, not to be trusted in a time when the attackers of Islam were also Christians. Many Copts emigrated to other countries where their hard-won ability to adapt to life under difficult circumstances must have stood them in good stead. Arts that had been refined in Egypt, weaving among them, may have thus been spread to Europe, contributing to the flowering of craftsmanship that occurred during the Medieval period. Some Coptic beliefs, too, may have traveled north. There is at least one piece of evidence for this possibility: in 1151 Bishop Seffrid of Chichester, England, was buried wearing a ring set with a stone engraved

with a Gnostic deity, Abraxas (Ward et al. 1981:61, no. 116), that is, almost certainly, Egyptian in origin.

Looking at Coptic decorative motifs in light of the foregoing discussion, certain facts stand out. The predominance of motifs derived from Classical antiquity over those with obvious Christian connotations support the supposition that paganism did not end in the first century after the birth of Christ or even later, with the Edict of Milan in the fourth century. Some pagan cults still had active supporters as late as the fifth century: the poet Nonnos of Panopolis who chronicled the life of Dionysus is an example. After the Arab conquest, Coptic textiles ornamented with figures derived from Greek myth continued to be woven. By this time the motifs may have been entirely decorative, but their long life, nearly a thousand years in Egypt, was most certainly extended by their connection with living beliefs for 500 years, a circumstance not commonly taken into account by early textile historians.

A second point to keep in mind when studying Coptic motifs is the dualism found in both pagan and Christian beliefs. It rose as an attempt to solve what was seen as ongoing conflicts between good and evil forces. The conflicts themselves were various— between order and disorder, civilization and barbarism, man's spiritual nature and his undeveloped, "natural" nature. In myths and in art derived from the myths, these conflicts were symbolized by battles between men and animals or between men and real or mythical beasts—dragons, centaurs, lions, boars—often of unusual size and attributes. Victory over evil or disorder could be symbolized by a man riding a horse or guiding a chariot. Figures engaged in such activities are commonly found decorating Coptic textiles. Also common are pairs of similar or identical human figures. These, too, could be expressions of duality or spiritual conflict.

The possible symbolism underlying certain motifs will be mentioned in the catalog entries for particular textiles. Much of this is entirely speculative, of course. However, the Copts held to their religious and philosophical beliefs with remarkable firmness, often showing themselves willing to suffer for the sake of their retention. The Copts must have prized their textiles, judging from the care and invention often lavished on their manufacture. It would be surprising, indeed, if these enthusiasms did not in some way overlap with the result that the thematic content of the ornamentation of the textiles deliberately includes references to matters of the spirit.

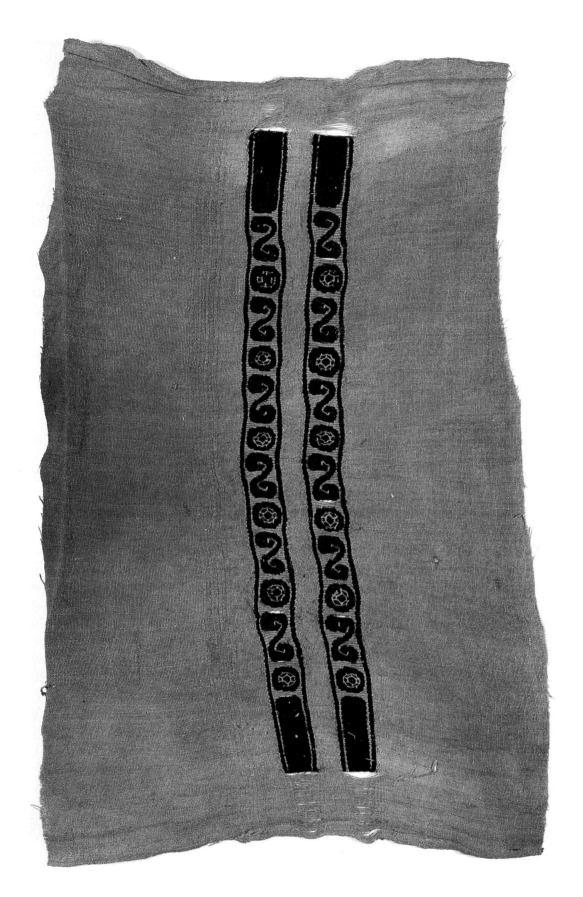

*2. Section Cut From a Tunic Sleeve  (See catalog entry, page 84)*     ↔

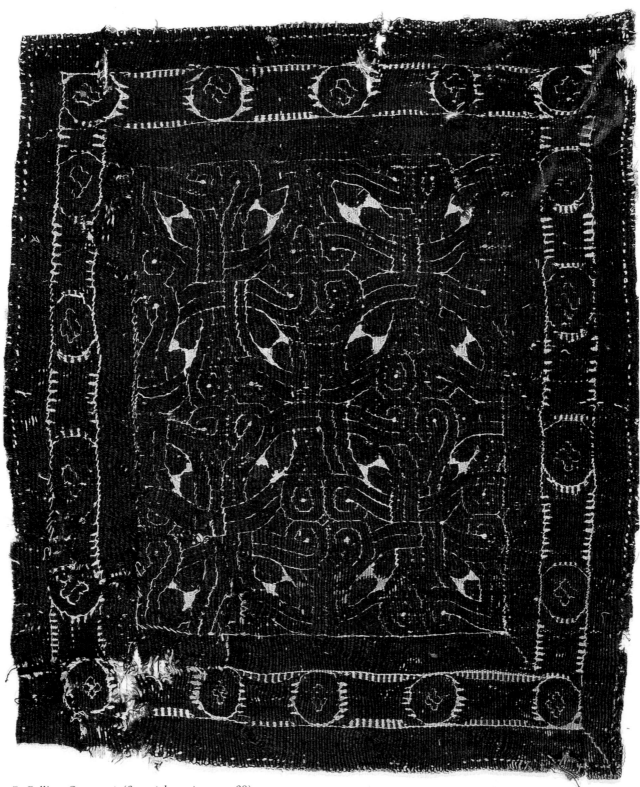

*7. Pallium Ornament  (See catalog entry, page 90)*

12. *Segment Cut From a Mantle or Curtain*  *(See catalog entry, page 98)*

*25. Fragment of a Tunic Sleeve  (See catalog entry, page 114)*  ↔

35.  *Fragment of a Tunic From Assyūt  (See catalog entry, page 128)*

36. *Square Decorative Garment Insert* *(See catalog entry, page 130)*

37. *Fragment of an Ecclesiastical Tapestry From Bawit(?)  (See catalog entry, page 130)*

40. *Garment Ornament  (See catalog entry, page 134)*

# V. SIGNIFICANT DATES:
## *The Historical Background*

HIS SECTION is a chronological list intended for quick reference. It combines the matters directly concerning textile design and production, most of them mentioned in the previous four sections, with important historical events that must have affected the lives of weavers if only indirectly.

### DYNASTIC EGYPT

**c. 2900 B.C.** First dynasty began. The technology for weaving fine linen textiles was already developed by this time, demonstrated by finds of textiles in the tomb of Zer at Abydos. One variety of domesticated linen was grown, *L. usitatissimun* L. (formerly called *Linum humile* Mill.).

**c. 2000 B.C.** Dynasty XI. Tomb of the Vizer Daga at Thebes. In it was discovered a mural painting showing a woman preparing a warp for a loom and two other women weaving on a horizontal loom pegged to the ground.

**c. 1990 B.C.** Dynasty XII. Tomb of Chnem-hotep at Beni Hasan. One of its paintings depicts a horizontal ground loom worked by two weavers.

**c. 1700 B.C.** Hyksos invaded Egypt. The Hyksos, a nomadic people of disputed origin, are believed to have introduced the high-warp loom and the weaving of brightly colored patterned textiles.

**c. 1425 B.C.** Dynasty XVIII. Tomb of Thot-nefer, a royal scribe, at Thebes. Painting showing two high-warp looms, one with two seated men working it, the other, smaller loom worked by one seated man.

**c. 1330 B.C.** End of Dynasty XVIII. Tomb of Nefer-hotep at Thebes. Painting of a weaver working at an upright loom on which is depicted a cloth with colored stripes near the edges.

**c. 1200 B.C.** Dynasty XX. Tomb of Nefer-

ronpet, superintendent of weaving at Thebes. Painting of a weaving room containing four looms, five weavers (one loom has two weavers working it), and two people preparing warp.

**c. 600 B.C.** Naucratis in the Delta founded. It became an important commercial center for Egypt, an early source of Greek influence, and a channel for the export of Egyptian goods, including textiles, to other parts of the Mediterranean.

**525 B.C.** Egypt came under Persian rule after the defeat of Psamtik III by Cambyses.

**c. 460–455 B.C.** Herodotus (2.35) observed and recorded the topsy-turvy ways of the Egyptians, including weavers, evidence that the Egyptians were unfamiliar with warp-weighted looms.

**333–332 B.C.** Alexander the Great conquered Egypt. Alexander paid homage to the native gods and was accepted as king of Egypt.

**332 B.C.** In the fall of this year Alexander founded Alexandria. The city became a major center for the production of fine textiles and other luxury goods. It was laid out as a Greek city according to a plan made by a Rhodian architect named Dinocrates.

**323 B.C.** On June 13, Alexander the Great died of malaria(?). His death marked the end of his plan to create a culturally integrated empire.

### PTOLEMAIC EGYPT

**305 B.C.** Ptolemy, son of Lagus, later called Ptolemy Soter, became king of Egypt and reigned until 283 B.C. He founded the Ptolemaic dynasty which survived until 30 B.C. Literary evidence indicates that the Ptolemies, following Greek customs, made lavish use of figured and patterned textiles, especially on festive occasions.

**285 B.C.** Reign of Ptolemy Philadelphus began. His reign lasted until 246, and during it the *Museion* of Alexandria was created. By this time an elaborate bureaucracy was in place, much of it connected with the regulation and taxation of textile production.

**257 B.C.** Pisicles inventoried Zenon's wardrobe (Hunt and Edgar 1932: 412–415), leaving to posterity an illustration of the nature and number of garments owned by a man of means. Zenon was estate manager for the finance minister of Ptolemy Philadelphus, and quantities of his business papers, many of them relating to textile production, are extant.

**250 B.C.** Two fictional (?) Greek matrons, Gorgo and Praxinoa, visited an Adonis shrine set up by Queen Arsinoë in the palace at Alexandria and admired the beautiful figured tapestries decorating it (Theocritus *Idyl XV*, Gow 1950).

**85 B.C.** The venerable city of Thebes in Upper Egypt destroyed as a result of a native uprising brought about by certain oppressive laws and actions of the Macedonian-Greek rulers.

**31 B.C.** Cleopatra and Antony defeated at the naval battle of Actium, which marked the end of the Ptolemaic dynasty.

**30 B.C.** Cleopatra committed suicide after having failed to persuade Octavian to fall in with her plans to restore the Ptolemaic Empire. Egypt became a province of Rome, but daily life for ordinary people was little changed.

## THE ROMAN PERIOD

**31 B.C.** Accession of Caesar Octavianus, termed Augustus, in 27 B.C.

**29 B.C.** The Temple of Janus closed and the Ara Pacis dedicated. Except for two brief civil wars in A.D. 69 and 193, during the 200 years after Augustus's death in A.D. 14 the Roman Empire flourished and was at peace. Augustus divided the Roman provinces between the emperor and the senate. He took charge of the unpacified provinces that needed military control, among them, Egypt. Augustus administered Egypt as a private estate, taking full advantage of the tax collection system established by the Ptolemies, and funneling the proceeds into the imperial

treasury. Except for meeting the demands of the tax collectors, life offered few challenges, and Egyptian culture became fixed, with stringently defined social classes.

**4 B.C.** Probable date of the birth of Jesus and of the flight into Egypt. This early adventure has special meaning for Egyptian Christians. Jesus is believed to have spent his childhood in Egypt. Scenes from the early years of Jesus decorate some Coptic textiles.

**A.D. 1** An anonymous housewife had a weaver in to weave a mantle, supplying him with food and beer during the process as well as a fee of 1 drachma, 2 obols for the completed mantle (Hunt and Edgar 1932:420–425).

**A.D. 30** In Jerusalem, Pontius Pilate sentenced Jesus, accused of sedition, to death.

**A.D. 40–49** According to tradition, John Mark visited Alexandria and found people, afflicted by the oppressive dullness of daily life, interested in his message. He may have produced an Egyptian-language version of his Gospel in addition to the ones he wrote in Greek and Latin.

**A.D. 64** In Rome, Emperor Nero put to death a number of Christians, blaming them for setting the fire that destroyed most of the city.

**A.D. 66** Anti-Christian riots in Alexandria instigated by Jews, angered because the Christians did not support the Jewish uprising against Rome.

**A.D. 68** Traditional date of John Mark's martyrdom in Alexandria at the hands of an angry mob of Serapis worshipers. John Mark and his Christian followers were celebrating Easter, which this year coincided with the festival of Serapis, and the two groups clashed.

**A.D. 80** Beginning of period when Gnosticism, a Christian cult with pagan antecedents, flourished in Egypt.

**A.D. 81–96** Isis-Serapis cult favored in Rome by Domitian. Although it originated in Egypt, this cult had only limited acceptance there, but was quite popular elsewhere.

**c. A.D. 98** Relief carved on a building of the Forum of Nerva; contains depictions of high-warp looms that may resemble contemporary Egyptian looms.

A.D. 130 Hadrian founded Antinoöpolis after a visit to Egypt. During his reign, 117–138, there was a revived interest in Greek art, especially in that of the Archaic period. Antinoöpolis later became famous for textiles woven in a realistic figured style that perhaps reflects the style of Hellenistic mosaics and mural paintings.

c. A.D. 150 Artemidorus of Ephesus wrote his *Oneicocritica*, which mentions both a horizontal and a vertical loom together.

A.D. 161–180 Reign of Marcus Aurelius. He was a proponent of Stoic philosophy. During his reign Stoicism reaches its highest point of refinement.

c. A.D. 175 A tomb built near Rome is decorated with a scene showing an upright loom, the latest ancient loom depiction detailed enough to be useful.

A.D. 183 Thonis was apprenticed to Heraclas, son of Sarapion, a weaver, for a period of five years (Hunt and Edgar 1932:40–45). Apprenticeship contracts, of which a number have survived, often provide important information about the textile industry.

A.D. 188 The reign of the 12th patriarch, Demetrius I (188–230), commenced. State-sponsored persecution of religious dissidents began.

A.D. 200 Culmination of attacks made on Gnosticism by a variety of Christian writers.

A.D. 202 Edict against Egyptian Christians was issued by Septimius Severus. It was intended to halt conversions. Those who refused to perform the token ceremony of burning incense before an imperial statue were put to death, usually by one of a variety of sadistic means.

A.D. 205–270 Plotinus of Assyūt became the greatest Neoplatonic philosopher of his time with a system echoing the religious doctrines of the local Christian priesthood.

A.D. 210 Approximate date for the writing of the Leiden Papyrus, which gives directions for various magical processes.

A.D. 211 Persecutions slackened after the death of Severus.

A.D. 218–222 Elagabalus reigned. Tradition credits this emperor with the introduction of an ancient Eastern garment, the dalmatic, to the Western world.

A.D. 227 Sassanid Empire and the revival of Zoroastrianism commenced. This monotheistic religion was founded by Zoroaster, a Persian who lived during the seventh century B.C. Some of the motifs that appear on Coptic textiles may derive from the symbols of this religion.

A.D. 235 The civilian government of Rome collapsed. Various army commanders vied for the position of emperor. Economic life was shattered.

A.D. 241–271 Shapur I reigned. He first favored Mani, the founder of Manichaean-ism, but later banished him. Mani postu-lated a dual godhead in which the forces of good were balanced by the forces of evil. Some of Mani's followers were Egyptian Gnostics with a dualist orientation.

A.D. 249–251 All Christians, not just particular individuals, intensely persecuted under the Roman emperor Decius. Emperor-worship was taken seriously, and refusing to make at least a token compliance was perilous. Thousands were killed.

A.D. 253–260 Under the emperor Vale-rian, Christians continued to be persecuted.

A.D. 256 Dura-Europos destroyed in Syria. Preserved in the ruins were a number of brightly-colored wool twill fragments, earlier than extant Coptic textiles but with similarities to them.

A.D. 260-268 Gallienus reigned. He issued an edict of religious tolerance in 262. The practices of Christianity were permitted and churches were allowed to open. Property was returned to Christians. This was a period of rebuilding and development. During this time the first hermit, Anthony of Coma (251–356) appeared. He later organ-ized monastic life, which became a major feature of Egyptian Christianity.

A.D. 268–284 A series of strong emperors managed to repel invaders and to restore order throughout the Roman Empire.

A.D. 273 Mani executed by order of Varahran I by crucifixion, like Jesus, accord-ing to tradition. The religion he founded, Manichaeanism, had a long life and often competed with Christianity for followers.

A.D. 284 Year One of the Coptic calendar and the start of the Era of Martyrs. The Coptic New Year's Day, September 11, coincides with the accession of the Emperor Diocletian. He recognized that rule of the empire had to be shared, and made other changes as well. At first Diocletian tried to emulate Augustus, but his problems were too different and too great. Heavy taxes and a rigid caste system made personal betterment almost impossible, especially in Egypt. The appeal of Christianity with its promise of a glorious life in the hereafter was never greater, and many converts were made.

**A.D. 294–295** Revolt occurred in Egypt. This rebellion was squelched in person by Diocletian, who besieged Alexandria and captured its leader, Achilleus.

**A.D. 296** Diocletian completely reformed the Roman coinage system and introduced the copper denarius.

**A.D. 298** Appollonia bought an expensive loom (Hunt and Edgar 1932:106–109) intended for Tarsian weaving. The bill of sale describes the loom. It could have been a low-warp loom with treadles, a new type of loom that eventually replaced the older high-warp looms for most purposes.

**A.D. 300** Around this time the *Papyrus Graecus Holmiensis* was written, or more precisely, assembled. Among its 154 recipes are 63 for the textile worker. These include recipes for dyes, mordants, and wool-cleaning agents.

**A.D. 301** Diocletian and his co-rulers issued an edict intended to limit the maximum prices that can be demanded for goods and services. Nearly 500 of the items listed in the extant text of the edict concern textiles or textile manufacture.

**A.D. 303** February 23. Diocletian, persuaded by his co-ruler, issued edicts for the destruction of Christian churches and literature, for the confiscation of Christian property, and for dismissing Christians from state offices. Meetings were forbidden under penalty of death.

**A.D. 305–313** Maximianus Daia reigned. Persecutions ceased in the west in 306 after one bloody year, but continued in Egypt until 313. The death toll for this ten-year-long massacre was enormous — 144,000 or perhaps as high as 800,000 — estimates vary.

**A.D. 313** Constantine proclaimed the Edict of Milan. It guaranteed general religious toleration and the restoration of confiscated property. It also gave churchmen the power to punish heretics physically. Constantine and members of his close family eventually became Christians, but originally they were all worshippers of Helios.

**A.D. 323** Christianity became the state religion and all pagan practices were forbidden, among them mummification. After this time the dead were buried fully clothed and wrapped in spare garments and domestic textiles. This change in burial practice contributed greatly to the preservation of textiles that had been used in everyday life.

**A.D. 324** Constantine became sole emperor over a reunited empire. His problems were many. Between 324 and 360 the denarius went from 4350 to the solidus to 4,600,000. (The solidus was a gold coin that weighed, at this time, 4.548 grams, 1/72 of the Roman pound [327.45 grams].)

**A.D. 325** The Council of Nicaea, during which Arianism, favored by Constantine, was defeated and condemned. Even so, Arianism continued to provide resources for the greatest metaphysical battle of the fourth century. At issue was the question of the Trinitarian unity. On one side was the Athanasian principle of consubstantiation (*homoousios*) in which the Son and Father were of the same essence, as against the Arian principle (*homoiousios*) in which the Son was only of like essence, begotten of the Father, but not equal.

**A.D. 330** Constantinople was dedicated by Constantine as his capital.

**A.D. 327** Constantine died on May 22.

**A.D. 337–360** Period of strife among the three sons of Constantine. The strongest, Constantius, favored Arianism.

**c. A.D. 350** An illuminated copy of the Æneid (The Vatican Virgil) was made, containing a sketchy depiction of Kirke working at a two-beamed upright loom.

**A.D. 361–363** Julian, known to history as the Apostate, reigned. Paganism was far from dead, and Julian rallied many supporters. Brief as his reign was, it had serious repercussions. The apprehensions of the Christians were aroused, they feared a pagan resurgence and a new era of persecution, and they reacted in ways that were often violent.

**A.D. 367** Athanasius, Archbishop of Alexandria, ordered a purge of all apocryphal books and books with heretical tendencies. This may be the time when the Nag Hammadi codices, a collection of writings largely Gnostic in content, were packed in a large jar and buried near the monastery of Saint Pachomius in the Thebaid region of Upper Egypt.

A.D. 379 Theodosius the Great ascended to the throne and proclaimed that Christianity again was the religion of the state. Pagans and believers in the Arian form of Christianity were persecuted.

A.D. 381 The Council of Constantinople firmly established the Nicene Creed as the accepted form of Christian belief.

A.D. 389 Patriarch Theophilus (385–412) leading a large mob, destroyed the Temple of Serapis at Canopus (a suburb of Alexandria).

A.D. 395 Death of Theodosius, who had divided his empire between his two sons, Arcadius and Honorius.

A.D. 410 Rome was sacked by Alaric, an event that caused shock throughout the known world.

A.D. 411 The chief Serapis temple destroyed by a mob along with a major part of the Ptolemaic Library. (Little of the library was left for the Arabs to burn, if indeed they actually committed this barbarism.) Again, the leader of the mob was Patriarch Theophilus. Other temples were destroyed as well.

A.D. 412–44 Cyril, later called Saint Cyril the Great, became patriarch. He formed a private army of militant monks, which he used to harass and destroy pagans and Jews in Alexandria and its environs. At the same time, Saint Shenute of Panopolis and his followers, no less violent in their methods, worked to eradicate paganism from the Thebaid, a stronghold of ancient beliefs, in Upper Egypt.

A.D. 415 Hypatia stoned to death. Saint Cyril is believed to have instigated this killing. A neoplatonist and a mathematician, Hypatia taught both pagans and Christians and was highly regarded by scholars of both persuasions.

A.D. 425 Priests of Isis still used demotic script at Philae.

A.D. 430 Saint Augustine of Hippo died. Before becoming converted to Christianity, Saint Augustine had explored Neoplatonic philosophy and the tenets of Manichaeanism.

A.D. 451 The Fourth Ecumenical Council at Chalcedon condemned the Monophysite doctrine of the Copts, which held that Jesus Christ was one person from two beings, God and man, and had one nature.

A.D. 452 The appointment of the Melkite Proterius as patriarch of the See of Alexandria in place of a native Egyptian. (The Melkites were Royalist Greeks who originated from Constantinople but obeyed Chalcedonian directives.) The Egyptians elected a patriarch of their own, a Monophysite.

A.D. 455 Approximate date for the birth of Nonnos at Panopolis (Chemmis) in the Thebaid. He wrote his poem on the life of Dionysus, really a collection of traditional stories about the god, shortly before the year 500. It paraphrases the meter and style of Saint John's Gospel. Christian scholars claimed Nonnos as one of their own belief, but it is quite possible that he was actually a follower of Dionysus, the principal deity of a late Antique cult related to Orphism. A number of Coptic textiles feature motifs that could pertain to this cult, evidence that indicates the continued popularity of Orphism.

A.D. 476 Barbarians completely overran the western part of the empire.

A.D. 493 Ostrogoths established a kingdom in Italy.

A.D. 502 Egypt suffered a severe famine.


## BYZANTINE EGYPT

A.D. 527 Accession of Emperor Justinian, who reigned until 565. Portraits of Justinian and Empress Theodora show them wearing garments made of beautifully decorated textiles. Some extant Coptic textiles resemble these. Paganism was officially ended again. Justinian closed the Temple of Isis at Philae and the Temple of Amon in the Siwa Oasis. Textiles with Isis motifs probably predate the closing of this temple. Justinian favored the Chalcedonian form of Christianity but Theodora was secretly a Monophysite. She did much to protect her fellow believers. Egypt became completely disorganized and religious differences became the basis for political divisions.

A.D. 541 The Melkite patriarch Apollinarius was nominated to the See of Alexandria. At the same time, he was invested with prefectural military powers in order to enforce matters concerning religion. Apollinarius eventually conducted a public massacre of unruly Monophysites.

A.D. 600 Around this date the Monastery of Epiphanius was founded. Excavations of the site uncovered structures that some identify as the remains of treadle pits for harness looms. Much weaving was done in monasteries. Monastic life was planned to be largely self-sufficient in order to minimize contact with the greater world. The difficulties of life in this period induced many to withdraw from it and to live apart as monks.

A.D. 610 Heraklius, a Byzantine general, usurped the crown and became emperor.

A.D. 619 Sassanian Persians invaded Egypt. They ruled until expelled by Heraklius in 627. Coptic textiles with Persian motifs appear.

A.D. 622 July 15. The Muslim era began on this date, according to tradition. However, historians believe the flight of Mohammed and his followers, which this date commemorates, took place several days earlier.

A.D. 626–658 Period of military struggles between Byzantines and Persians and Muslim Arabs.

A.D. 627 The Emperor Heraklius recovered the Holy Cross and returned it to Jerusalem. This event may have inspired the invention of the motif of the jeweled cross, a common motif in art of the Byzantine period that also appears on Coptic textiles. It signifies the First Coming.

A.D. 630 Heraklius elevated the Melkite Cyrus to Patriarch of Alexandria and Imperial Prefect of Egypt. His orders were to bring all Copts to the Chalcedonian brand of faith by any means. For 10 years Cyrus went about this in a manner totally lacking in subtlety or mercy. Coptic churchmen of every degree were tried and tortured. Large numbers of them were killed. Ten years of Cyrus's activities made Byzantine rule and all other things Byzantine extremely unpopular. A division was thus created not only in religion but also in language, literature, and art. So hated was Byzantium that the Copts did little to assist Cyrus in defending Egypt when the Arab attackers arrived.

A.D. 632 Mohammed died. His death was followed almost immediately by Arab attacks on neighboring countries, Persia, Syria, and the Byzantine Empire.

## MUSLIM EGYPT

A.D. 640 A general of Caliph Omar, 'Amr ibn al-'As conquered Egypt. The Arab rulers did not differentiate among the varieties of Christian—Monophysite, Monothelite, or Melkite. This was a relief to the Monophysite Copts who had been living in terror and civil disability. For a time, even though under Arab rule, the Copts experienced a revival of religion, literature, and art, all nearly free of Greek, actually Byzantine, influences. Weaving in particular flourished.

A.D. 641 By this year over 90 percent of the Egyptian population was Christian. A number of Copts gradually converted to Islam in order to be spared the heavy taxes demanded of Christians. The drop in tax revenues became marked, and some Muslim viceroys, aware of the monetary loss to the state these lost revenues caused, went so far as to discourage conversions.

A.D. 658-750 Umayyad dynasty was established in Damascus. Egypt was ruled by governors.

A.D. 705 The Umayyad Viceroy made Arabic the official language for all state transactions.

A.D. 726 Start of Iconclastic controversy. Leo III, pious founder of the Isaurian dynasty of Byzantium, attempted to correct certain excesses that had crept into Christian worship and life-style. One of his actions in this connection was to forbid image-worship.

A.D. 731 Pope Gregory III responded by excommunicating all Iconoclasts. A period of struggle followed, in some cases involving extreme persecutions on the part of the Iconoclasts. It is not clear how this controversy affected Coptic Christians, but some Coptic textiles of the period have motifs that are schematic to the point of being barely recognizable as depictions of living subjects.

A.D. 750 'Abbassid dynasty was founded at Baghdad. The Copts, oppressed and heavily taxed, staged a series of revolts. At this time Copts spoke Arabic, and Coptic survived principally as the language of religious ritual.

A.D. 775–785 Caliphate of al-Mahdi. Gnostic-Manichaeans, in particular, were subjects of persecution.

A.D. 843 The veneration of images by Christians was restored.

A.D. 868–905 Tulunid dynasty. This was the first independant Muslim dynasty in Egypt, during which was built the great Ibn Tulun mosque in Cairo, designed by a Christian architect, Ibn Katib. He is thought to have invented the pointed arch featured in this structure long before it was discovered by European architects in the Medieval period. A possibly apocryphal explanation for the invention claims that it made unnecessary the cannibalization of the nave columns of Christian churches (many of which had earlier been taken from pagan structures).

A.D. 935-969 Ikhshidid dynasty. Coptic Christians were required to wear yellow garments: late textiles with yellow or dark orange grounds may derive from this period. The gradual abandonment of Coptic towns and monasteries began. The inhabitants dispersed, in some instances to other countries.

A.D. 968 Fatimid dynasty commenced. The Fatimid caliphs invaded Egypt from Tunisia and founded Cairo as their capital city in 969. Cairo became the center of an empire that extended from Morocco to Syria. Under the Fatimids, Egypt became a brilliant center of Muslim culture. The early caliphs were particularly tolerant toward both Copts and Jews, a feeling that was not shared by lower-class Muslims, and Coptic literacy and craftsmanship were highly valued. Coptic weavers were very active, but the design motifs used for textiles changed, becoming ever more Islamic in character. During the end of the ninth century and the beginning of the tenth there was a period of persecution of both Jews and Christians under Caliph al-Hakim who was, it is suspected, insane. He disappeared under mysterious circumstances, to the relief of nearly everybody. Religious liberty was restored, but the Fatimid dynasty was severely weakened and was soon beset by many internal problems.

A.D. 1065 Egypt experienced drought, famine, and plague.

A.D. 1099 Baldwin failed in an attempt to conquor Egypt during the First Crusade.

A.D. 1151 In England, Bishop Seffrid of Chichester was buried wearing a ring set with a Gnostic gem. Other such engraved gems have been found in various places in Europe, perhaps carried there by Copts emigrating from Egypt.

A.D. 1168 The city of al-Fustat was deliberately burned, to prevent it from being used as a military base by the Crusaders during their attempt to conquer Egypt. It burned for 54 days. The people who had lived there were left destitute. It is believed that al-Fustat had a large Coptic population. The whole period of the Crusades was a time of unmitagated disaster for the Copts. The Muslims considered them to be Christians, but the Crusaders considered them heretics.

A.D. 1169 Salah el Din, or Saladin, founded the Ayyubid Dynasty. At first Copts were dismissed from office and humilated by being forced to wear distinctive dress and to refrain from riding horses. After Saladin's conquest of the Kingdom of Jerusalem of the Crusaders in 1187, a more tolerant attitude prevailed toward the Copts. Even so, Copts continued to migrate to other parts of the known world, taking their specialized skills with them.

c. A.D. 1250 An English manuscript, now at Cambridge, was decorated with a miniature that shows a nude man with curly hair and a scant beard working a fully developed low-warp loom. The style of his hair and beard has a Coptic appearance, and it is not improbable that the model was a Copt who had fled his native land. From this time foreward, low-warp looms were used for nearly all but certain highly specialized forms of textiles such as large wall hangings in tapestry weave.

# VI. THE RIETZ COPTIC TEXTILES:
## An Illustrated Catalog

THE INDIVIDUAL TEXTILES in the Carl Austin Rietz Coptic Textile Collection are catalogued as follows: first, a brief descriptive title, identifying, if only tentatively, the purpose originally served by the textile and giving an indication of its present condition. The section *colors and design* is next, followed by *materials and construction*. Except for one fragment of a silk textile, textiles are made of linen and wool combined, or of wool by itself. All the yarn is S-twist. In a few examples, which are identified, yarn that has been doubled and given a Z-twist is used for warp. The weave is noted, commonly rep or tabby, with tapestry ornament. The average thread count, that is, the number of warps and wefts in one typical square centimeter, is given, always the warp count is the first of the two numbers. The warp measurement is first, too, in the *dimensions* section. Most of the pieces are irregular in the extreme, so the measurements are, of necessity, approximate. *Related examples* are cited for some specimens, for purposes of dating and perhaps identifying the original form of the related Rietz piece. An estimated *date* comes next, followed by the *accession number*. The final section, *remarks*, is intended to give background information about the piece, including speculations about its original form and the possible significance of any design motifs.

---

The textiles in this group are the earliest in the collection and belong to the period dominated by Rome. A number of them represent types of garments that could have indicated social rank or would have been appropriate wear for persons with high positions in the extensive bureaucracy of the period.

*1. Square Emblem Cut from a Pallium(?)*

*Colors and design:* The square has a red-purple ground with a pattern worked in white. The design consists of a border of stylized grape leaves surrounding a center block composed of four similar grape leaves. At the top and bottom of the square is a cable pattern that degenerates at the sides, becoming a sketchy design suggesting chicken scratches.

*Materials and construction:* The little that remains of the ground was woven in linen rep, 22 x 9. The background of the emblem was woven in tapestry, wool weft on grouped linen warps, 16 x 13. The details of the design were worked in a combination of embroidery and weft floats. The tapestry background of the emblem was woven in evenly placed straight shots; the weft-float surface pattern was worked over it as the background weaving progressed.

1. *Square Emblem Cut from a Pallium(?)*

*Dimensions:* 19 x 18 cm.

*Date:* Late third or early fourth century.

*Accession number:* 389-2397.

*Remarks:* The pallium, as it is shown worn by ordinary men in Early Christian art, is commonly decorated with square purple emblems. Such emblems may have signified social position or office. The simple design of this specimen might have been intended to appeal to a follower of one of the more austere schools of philosophy.

---

## 2. Section Cut from a Tunic Sleeve

*(Color plate, page 67)*

*Colors and design:* The tan ground, originally white, bears two bands decorated with dark purple, double-scroll motifs alternating with small roundels. Each roundel is ornamented with a small rosette.

*Materials and construction:* The ground is linen rep, 24 x 15, the inserts wool tapestry, 10 x 26, with weft-float ornament. Both right and left selvedges are preserved. The weaving of the ornamental motifs appears to have started at the left, and each motif was completed before the next one was started. Above the decorated bands is a *shadow* band composed of four shots of bundled weft. The method of inserting weft floats can be clearly seen on the reverse side.

*Dimensions:* 22 x 34 cm.

*Date:* Early fourth century.

*Accession number:* 389-2402.

*Remarks:* White tunics with plain or simply ornamented, double purple sleeve bands occur frequently in Early Christian art. Usually the tunics also carried matching bands descending vertically from the shoulders on both the front and the back. Like the preceding specimen, the modest design might have been considered suitable for a person of philosophical bent.

---

## 3. Oval Dress Ornament

*Colors and design:* The ornament is an *orbiculum* with a linear pattern of diagonally-placed meander bands, delineated in tan on a red-purple ground.

*Materials and construction:* The motif was woven in the tapestry technique, in fine wool yarn on paired linen warps, 8 x 50. The surface patterning was created from weft floats of undyed linen thread. The ground of the motif was woven in sections that conform to the main lines of the surface patterning.

*Dimensions:* 18.5 x 16.5 cm.

*Related examples:* Paris, Louvre (Du Bourguet 1964, no. A 23).

*Date:* Late third or early fourth century.

*Accession number:* 389-2398.

*Remarks:* Tunics in Early Christian and Byzantine art were often decorated with matching sets of round, square, or oval motifs, one motif over each shoulder and two others placed in the region of the knees. It is possible that they were intended to guard the vital arm and knee joints from real or imagined dangers. The delicate, restrained linear decoration is typical of the period.

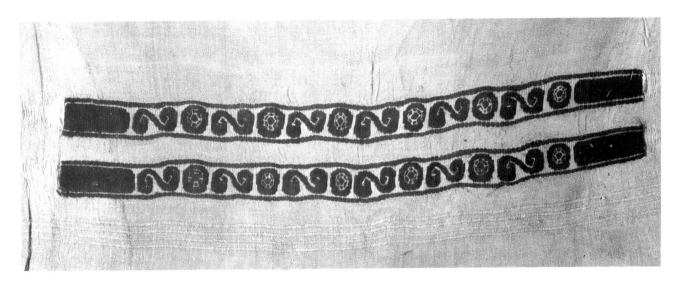

2. *Section Cut from a Tunic Sleeve*

3. *Oval Dress Ornament*

## 4. Tapestry Insert Cut from a Linen Textile

*Colors and design:* The design is a dark, purple-tinged brown, eight-pointed star composed of two separate, never-ending knots, interlaced together. The bands of the interlace are double; one half is plain, the other filled with a spiral-wave design. The square and triangular spaces not covered by the bands are filled with trefoils; the octagon in the middle is filled with an allover design of lozenges. What little remains of the ground is cream-colored and the patterning is tan.

*Materials and construction:* The insert is made from wool and linen wefts woven on grouped linen warps, 6 x 58, with weft-float patterning in two sizes of linen yarn. Originally part of a large (?) linen textile, now all that remains is this tapestry insert. It was woven in segments, horizontal and vertical bars and triangles. The outlines of these forms correspond to the lines of the interlace and its filler motifs. Slits were whip-stitched closed with linen yarn, an application that is at once practical and decorative. The wool yarn may have been purple originally. Color changes indicate that at least two different dye lots of yarn were used. These changes also testify to the section-by-section method of weaving described.

*Dimensions:* 29 x 30 cm.

*Related examples:* Paris, Louvre AC 150 (Du Bourguet 1964, no. A 11) and Washington D.C., Textile Museum 71.104 (Trilling 1982, no. 82).

*Date:* First half of the fourth century.

*Accession number:* 389-2377.

*Remarks:* A patch pasted on the back in recent times could be a scrap of the original linen that surrounded the insert. The intact textile may have been an altar cloth. The southern lunette of the sanctuary of San Vitale, Ravenna, Italy contains a mosaic depicting the sacrifices of Abel and Melchizedek (Grabar 1966:156). The cloth on their altar is ornamented with an eight-pointed star very similar in form to the Rietz specimen. Complex interlace patterns are almost universally believed to have protective powers, guarding against the evil eye. The tendency when looking at such a pattern is to trace the path of the interlace visually, thus keeping the eye moving. (It was the fixed stare that was considered dangerous.) Some ancient beliefs held that even sacred things needed protection from the evil eye.

## 5. Pair of Tunic Clavi Sewn Together to Form a Wide Band

*Colors and design:* The clavi are dull purple bands with scalloped edges. Their decoration consists of a small, undulating ladder band down the centers with filler-motifs of circles in two sizes. The larger circles contain various ornaments: circles with dot-clusters, rings of dots, four-petaled rosettes, hooked crosses, and a motif suggesting a laurel wreath.

*Materials and construction:* The ground is linen rep, 28 x 20; the clavi are woven in tapestry, wool and linen weft on grouped linen warps, 9 x 68. The design of the bands is carried out principally in an erratic weft-float technique.

*Dimensions:* 14 x 71 cm.

*Related example:* Paris, Louvre X4392 (Du Bourguet 1964).

*Date:* Fourth century.

*Accession number:* 389-2413.

*Remarks:* The piece is composed of two bands sewn together, possibly in antiquity. One band retains a strip of rep along one edge and a portion of the selvedge. The tunic to which the clavi belonged must have been a sober and dignified garment made in the best Roman tradition.

4. *Tapestry Insert Cut from a Linen Textile*

5. *Pair of Tunic Clavi Sewn Together to Form a Wide Band*

## 6. Oval Pallium Ornament

*Colors and design:* The design is based upon a slightly distorted dark purple circle with a tan, originally white, spiral-wave border. Its center is filled with a grid design. Alternate intersections of the grid lines are decorated with four-petaled rosettes. Figure-eight motifs occupy the grid rectangles.

*Materials and construction:* The ground has been completely removed; it was most probably linen rep. The ornament itself is tapestry, wool and linen weft on linen warp, 8 x 28. There is an extraordinary displacement of warp threads. The fine linear details of the design were worked in weft floats, the solid areas were carried out in tapestry.

*Dimensions:* 34 x 35.7 cm.

*Related example:* Moscow, Pushkin Museum inv. #362 (Shurinova 1967:64).

*Date:* Fourth century.

*Accession number:* 389-2407.

*Remarks:* The warp displacement suggests that this piece was woven on a warp-weighted loom. The warp-weighted loom was retained by the Romans for weaving the garments worn by brides and those worn by young men when they came of age. Also, special types of weaving techniques are easier to carry out on this most ancient loom, a fact which might account for its continued preservation. The handsome appearance of this roundel, with its fine linear pattern, would certainly make it an appropriate decoration for a garment worn during a serious, formal ceremony.

*Close-up of segment of Number 6. Abrupt changes in the warp direction are clearly visible in the border region.*

6. *Oval Pallium Ornament*

## 7. Pallium Ornament

*(Color plate, page 68)*

*Colors and design:* The dark purple rectangle has a wide border of two plain bands edging a third band decorated with widely spaced circles. The circles contain four-petaled rosette filler-motifs. In the center of the rectangle is an elaborate curvilinear geometric interlace.

*Materials and construction:* The rectangle was worked in wool and linen on grouped linen warps, 6 x 40. The weave is tapestry. The lines of the design were carried out in weft floats and embroidery done during the course of the weaving.

*Dimensions:* 39 x 34 cm.

*Date:* Late fourth or early fifth century.

*Accession number:* 389-2406.

*Remarks:* In antiquity, this piece was cut from the garment it decorated originally and applied to another. White *pallia* ornamented with large purple rectangles were worn by court officials in late antique times, as evidenced by works of art; for example, the apse mosaic of the emperor Justinian and his court in San Vitale, Ravenna, Italy (Grabar 1966:158–164; Paolucci 1978:46, 47, 50, 51). The Rietz example is earlier, judging from the style of the interlace design. The interlace design, like that of Number 4, may have been intended to avert, or divert, the evil eye, protecting the wearer of the ornament from its baleful effects. A highly placed official would need such protection, given the rough nature of the politics of the period.

*Three techniques: tapestry, ressort, and embroidery, are skillfully combined in the decoration of Number 7.*

*7. Pallium Ornament*

## 8. Rectangle Cut from a Mantle(?)

*Colors and design:* The principal motif is a star, dark purple on a plain ground, originally white but now discolored. The eight-pointed star was constructed from two overlapping squares. The top square has a cable pattern border and a center roundel containing an intricate knot pattern delineated in linen thread. The corners contain ivy leaves and tendrils worked in two colors of yarn, saffron and cream. The colors were woven in separate shots, two saffron, one cream, and repeat. The small roundel in the center was worked in the same way and in the same colors. Only the corners of the bottom square are visible—they contain vine leaves. From one of these depends, or extends, a rinceau band with a vase motif at the end.

*Materials and construction:* The ground is linen rep, 18–26 x 9; the motif is tapestry, wool and linen weft on grouped linen warps, 5 x 36. The surface of the tapestry motif is ornamented in weft-float patterning carried out in two gauges of linen yarn. The piece retains one selvedge, most probably the right-hand one. The sequence of weaving appears to have been as follows: (1) An area of rep was woven up to the bottom of the main motif. (2) Warps to be used for the tapestry portions were selected and a second set of heddles put in place. In doing this, the selected warps were doubled or tripled, in no obvious sequence, and the unneeded warps left to float at the back. (3) Woven next were a few centimeters of tapestry, complete with weft-float ornament. (4) Concurrent with the weaving of the tapestry, a corresponding number of centimeters of rep were woven, filling the space on either side of the tapestry insert. The shots for the rep cross the warp in a straight line and pass under the tapestry insert and behind the unused warps. A number of these are still extant; others appear to have been cut away. Small, irregular spaces around the tapestry inserts are filled in with tapestry worked in the same linen yarn used for the rep portions of the piece in order to make these filler areas less conspicuous. (5) Steps 3 and 4 were repeated until the tapestry insert was completed. After the shape of the insert was established, the weaver appears to have woven the tapestry in sections in order to define the inner forms of the design; for example, the two lower corners of the square section were worked slightly ahead of the center roundel, building up an arc into which the center roundel fits. This helps retain the symmetry of the roundel, always in danger of becoming an oval under the downward action of the beater as the weft is compressed.

*Dimensions:* 33 x 54 cm.

*Related examples:* Paris, Louvre AC 181 (Du Bourguet 1964) and Moscow, Pushkin Museum inv. #320 (Shurinova 1967:54).

*Date:* Fifth century.

*Accession number:* 389-2376.

*Remarks:* A star motif of identical form decorates the mantle of the principal court lady of the empress Theodora shown in the sixth-century apse mosaic of San Vitale, Ravenna, Italy. The Rietz textile may have been part of a similar, though earlier, woman's mantle. Note the protective interlace in the middle, here relegated to a relatively minor part of the design. The ivy leaves are a Classical motif that refers sometimes to the god Dionysus and his maenad followers, and sometimes to his follower, Orpheus, around whom an important cult developed in the late Roman period. Orphism is related to Pythagoreanism, which holds that numbers and geometric constructions have esoteric meanings and powers. Some late Roman or Coptic geometric ornaments may have been inspired by Pythagorean philosophy.

8. *Rectangle Cut from a Mantle(?)*

*The use of grouped linen warps for the tapestry portions of a two-fiber textile are clearly visible in Number 8 where the wool weft has disintegrated.*

## 9. Piece Cut from a Woman's Mantle or Veil

*Colors and design:* The piece is decorated with four dark purple squares symmetrically arranged on a plain, light tan ground. The squares are patterned with geometric designs worked in tan.

*Materials and construction:* The ground is linen rep, 26 x 20, the tapestry squares are wool on linen warp. The yarn is fine and so densely packed that the thread count cannot be determined. The weft-float patterning of the surface was worked in two gauges of linen yarn. The rep ground has fringed edges and decorative ridges made from groups of bundled weft yarns placed at intervals. The sequence is as follows, from one preserved edge to the other: fringe, 2 cm, plain weave, 2 cm. In the center of this latter is a ridge composed of four shots of bundled wefts. Next is 2 cm of bare warp followed by 1 cm of plain weave. Last there is a group of ridges about 2 cm. wide containing three smaller groups, each formed from three shots of bundled weft. After this is 59 cm of plain weave, and then the edge treatment is repeated in reverse, ending with fringe. The other two edges have been cut

*9. Piece Cut from a Woman's Mantle or Veil*

with shears, most certainly in recent times. The tapestry squares are approximately 13 x 13 cm and are placed in the corners of an imaginary square 48 cm on a side. Their decoration was precisely worked in two gauges of natural-color linen yarn. They originally were part of a linen textile that was slightly coarser than the one they now decorate. The cut edges were neatly turned under and the squares whip-stitched in place. At some point in this operation the cloth behind the squares was trimmed away.

*Dimensions:* 73 x 69 cm.

*Date:* Late fourth or early fifth century.

*Accession number:* 389-2375.

*Remarks:* Fringed veils sparsely ornamented with colored squares are worn by the female martyrs shown in procession on the upper left side of the nave of Sant'Appollinare Nuovo, Ravenna, Italy; this depiction lends support to the identification of the Rietz fragment as part of a woman's garment (Paolucci 1978:58).

*One of the squares (lower left corner) was cut from an older textile and appliquéd to Number 9.*

## 10. Tunic Sleeve Ornament

*Colors and design:* The ornament consists of two dark purple bands, each bearing an identical angular knot interlace. Between the bands is a row of two varieties of symmetrical cartouches, dark purple in color. The ground is tan linen rep.

*Materials and construction:* The linen rep ground has a count of 13 x 8, and is ornamented with a ridged band made from three shots of bundled wefts. The tapestry insert was woven in wool and linen weft on linen warp, 11 x 54, in a normal tapestry weave with weft-float ornamentation.

*Dimensions:* Sleeve ornament, 10 x 25 cm; backing cloth, 33 x 23 cm.

*Date:* Fifth century (?)

*Accession number:* 389-2403.

*Remarks:* This sleeve ornament was reused in antiquity. At present, it is lightly glued to the plain rep textile. This latter is ancient, and may be part of the tunic to which the sleeve ornament last belonged.

---

## 11. Pallium Fragment

*Colors and design:* The fragment has a tan ground and a large, purplish black roundel. The roundel has a border of small circles separated by pairs of smaller circles. Its center is filled by regularly spaced clusters of nine dots each.

*Materials and construction:* The entire fragment is weft loop pile carried out in linen and wool, 20 x 11, on a linen warp. Every fourth shot in the area of the motif is a weft bundle. Dyed wool threads added to the motif area form the colored pile. Every seventh and eighth shot is a weft bundle but only the eighth shot provides pile. The pile was formed by looping sections of the weft around a smooth rod. The size of the rod was determined by the depth of pile desired.

*Dimensions:* 55 x 58 cm.

*Date:* Fifth or early sixth century.

*Accession number:* 389-2583.

*Remarks:* As mentioned earlier, white pallia with large purple medallions were worn by dignitaries of church and state in the fifth and sixth centuries. Wear marks on this example indicate that it may have been worn inside-out, perhaps after having been discarded by the original, distinguished owner, or used as a chair or couch cover. The technique for weaving a textile with a pile surface evolved in Dynastic Egypt. Riefstahl cites an eleventh-dynasty example found at Deir el-Bahri (1944:17, fig. 19), which already shows a perfect grasp of the method. The technique is an important one for the region. See Bellinger (1956).

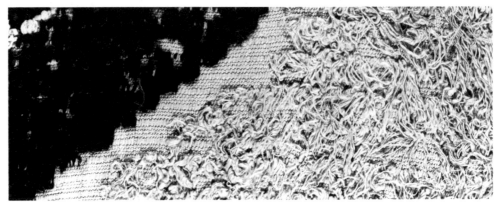

*The pile surface of Number 11 is velvet-like in areas with wool weft, rougher, like bath-toweling, in the all-linen portion.*

*10. Tunic Sleeve Ornament*

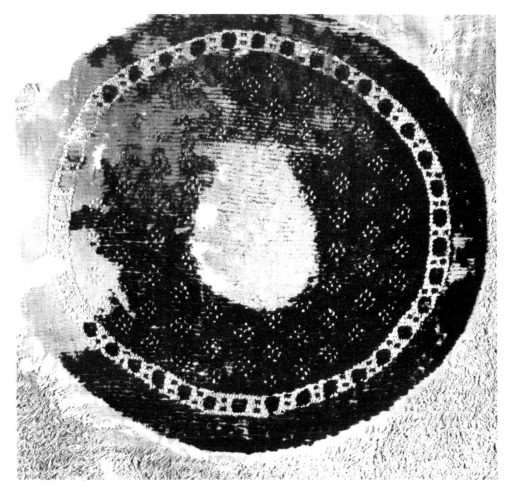

*11. Pallium Fragment*

## 12. Segment Cut from a Mantle or Curtain

*(Color plate, page 69)*

*Colors and design:* The plain, off-white ground is ornamented with a broad purple band and three narrow ones. The broad band has wide borders of double rinceau and a center with a knot interlace. The narrow bands are plain.

*Materials and construction:* The ground is linen rep, 20 x 11, the broad band is tapestry, wool and linen weft, linen warp, 6 x 52, with weft-float patterning. In the tapestery areas the weft has been deliberately displaced in order to follow the curves of the design. The bottom of the piece ends in warp fringe: above it is a section of bare warp.

*Dimensions:* 57.5 x 44 cm.

*Date:* Fifth century.

*Accession number:* 389-2421.

*Remarks:* The color of the wool yarn appears to be especially well preserved; this specimen gives a good idea of the purple and white color scheme favored for Coptic textiles of the early period.

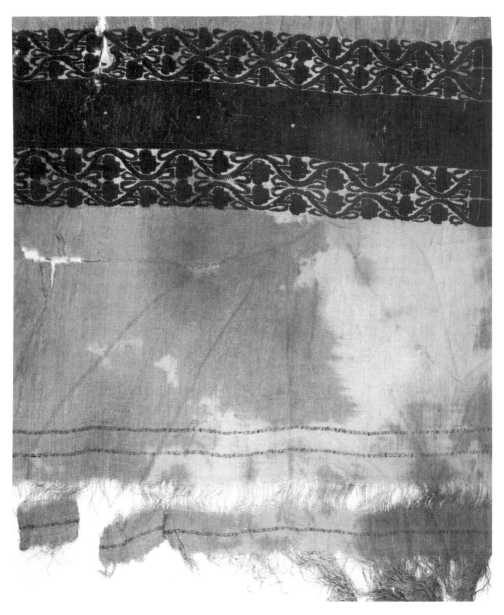

*12. Segment Cut from a Mantle or Tunic*

**13. Square Cut from a Woman's Tunic**

*Colors and design:* A formal, monochrome rinceau with filler-motifs, originally purple but now brown, decorates this piece. Three of its roundels contain symmetrical plants, three others animals. Two of the animals are hounds and one is a lion. The backgrounds of the animals are shaded; backgrounds of the plants, plain. Leaves, or possibly lotus pods, sprout from the vine stalks. The leaves of the small plants resemble vine leaves.

*Materials and construction:* The linen tabby ground, 16 x 16, has tapestry inserts woven in wool on grouped linen warps, 9 x 48. The weaving reflects considerable skill—the threads are fine and placed with precision.

*Dimensions:* 17.3 x 18.5 cm.

*Related example:* An entire garment in Moscow, Pushkin Museum inv. # 5823 (Shurinova 1967:5).

*Date:* Late fourth or early fifth century.

*Accession number:* 389-2394.

Remarks: The piece could be a part of a garment resembling the tunic in the Pushkin Collection, cited above, which is ornamented with motifs nearly identical to those of the Rietz specimen. The Moscow tunic has been identified as a woman's dress. From depictions in art it appears that the garments of women were more extensively decorated than those of men and were more likely to feature figured or floral motifs in their decoration.

13. *Square Cut from a Woman's Tunic*

## 14. Garment Ornament

*Colors and design:* The ornament is rendered in brown on a beige ground. It is square with a reverse scallop border around the edge. In the center is a small square with a lion motif. The space between the outer and inner square is filled with an elaborate lozenge pattern.

*Materials and construction:* The weaving was done in a normal tapestry technique with wool and linen wefts on paired linen warps, 9 x 52. Weft floats were used to indicate details.

*Dimensions:* 12.5 x 12 cm.

*Date:* Early fifth century.

*Accession number:* 389-2586.

*Remarks:* The piece was reused in antiquity, a common practice that illustrates the value placed on textile decoration. Lions have many symbolic meanings, some good, some evil. The Greek hero Herakles wore the pelt of the nearly invulnerable Nemean lion, a trophy he gained from the first of his 12 labors. The animal had a hide so tough it could only be killed by strangling; weapons could not penetrate it. The pelt of this lion became a symbol of the hero, who himself was sometimes given the surname "soter," which means savior. The depiction of a lion could thus refer to invulnerability, salvation, or both. Since the lion was also the symbol of Saint Mark, Evangelist and first patriarch of the church in Egypt, the motif of a lion could be worn by either a pagan or a Christian with perfect confidence in its efficacy.

## 15. Fragment of a Clavus

*Colors and design:* The clavus has a tan ground, originally white, and is decorated with an inhabited rinceau worked in light brown. The inhabitants are running animals—a hare, a lion, and an antelope.

*Materials and construction:* The basic weave is linen rep, 20 x 10, with a wool and linen tapestry insert woven on grouped warps, 7 x 32. The tapestry wefts are curved to help define the design.

*Dimensions:* 11 x 32.2 cm.

*Related examples:* An entire tunic with similar motifs is in London, Victoria and Albert Museum (Kendrick 1920:41, pl. 2).

*Date:* Fifth century.

*Accession number:* 389-2425.

*Remarks:* Scroll motifs in the form of leafy vines incorporating various zoomorphic motifs have late antique origins but continued to be popular in Early Christian and Medieval art. Running animals sometimes symbolize a hunt, the assumption being that something or someone is chasing them. The hunt, in turn, has its symbolism: the chase refers to the attempt to drive out various evils from an individual's life and psyche. Note that a lion in this context has a very different meaning than the isolated lion in the preceding example, Number 14.

14. *Garment Ornament*

15. *Fragment of a Clavus*

## 16. Tunic Sleeve Band Fragment

*Colors and design:* The decorated area is occupied by dark, brownish purple figures and motifs on a dull yellow ground. The band has crenellated ends and reverse-arcade side borders. At each end is the figure of a man, nude except for a diagonal belt and a long scarf, with one hand raised as if in a salute. Between the men are two lions, facing in opposite directions.

*Materials and construction:* The fragment is woven in a normal tapestry technique, 9 x 30–40, entirely in wool.

*Dimensions:* 9 x 28 cm.

*Date:* Fifth century.

*Accession number:* 389-2426.

*Remarks:* This is a sophisticated version of a very common Coptic textile motif that combines nude warriors (identified as such by sword-belts) and lions. The nudity of the warriors signifies that their battle is one of the spirit, a fight with the bestial side of their natures, symbolized here by the lions. The unnatural orientation of the lions in relation to the warriors is typical of the large class of Coptic textiles to which this example belongs. This design feature is also found on some drawloom textiles of the fifth century (Trilling 1982, no. 108). On these textiles, the position of the animals could have been dictated by certain technical limitations of the drawloom. The tapestry pieces with lions or other quadrupeds placed in a vertical position may derive from designs intended for drawloom weaving or from actual textiles woven on this loom.

---

The textiles in this group are reportedly from Shaikh Abada, or El Sheik Abara—the Arabic name for the site is transliterated variously. The ancient city was named Antinoöpolis after a beautiful Greek youth who drowned near there. It was founded in his memory by the emperor Hadrian around A.D. 13. A major weaving center in antiquity, some of its products have a classical flavor that may derive from Hadrian's interest in early Greek art. The archaic style of Greece was revived during his reign. Later, in the Christian period, Antinoöpolis became the site of a famous monastery founded by Saint Samuel. While it is impossible to place total reliance on antique dealers' attributions, the textiles in this group have similarities that make a common source believable. It is assumed that Rietz purchased them as a group, perhaps from a dealer in the vicinity.

## 17. Square Tunic Ornament

*(Illustrated on page 105)*

*Colors and design:* The ground is tan, the ornament dull purple and cream. The design is based upon a square. This has a reversed arcade border and smaller square in its center with a cruciform-knot filler motif. The remainder of the basic square is filled with four gammulae, two of them decorated with filler motifs of disks and fish-form blobs, two with a pattern composed of cruciform rosettes.

*Materials and construction:* The technique is tapestry on grouped linen warps with wool and linen weft, 11 x 48. Some of the ornament is done in weft floats.

*Dimensions:* 13 x 11 cm.

*Date:* Fifth century.

*Accession number:* 389-2395.

*Remarks:* The knot motif used on this piece may be a form of cross. The design organization is the same as that of the squares on Number 9, but the filler motifs are much coarser.

16. *Tunic Sleeve Band Fragment* ←→

## 18. Tunic Ornament

*Colors and design:* The square design is worked in brown on a beige background. The center motif is a small dove framed by a square composed of eight circles, each with a filler motif of an equal-armed cross. Around the edge is a spiral-wave border.

*Materials and construction:* The foundation is linen tabby, 12 x 12. The wool and linen tapestry ornament was woven on paired warps, 9 x 60. The square ornament was either made separately or cut from another, possibly worn-out, garment. The edges are turned under and the piece neatly whip-stitched to the linen tabby foundation.

*Dimensions:* 10 x 9 cm.

*Date:* Fifth century.

*Accession number* 389-2428.

*Remarks:* Doves, in Early Christian art, symbolize the Holy Ghost and also, because of the dove in the Noah story, deliverance from danger. This piece is a straightforward example of a Coptic textile with a Christian motif.

*18. Tunic Ornament*

17.  Square Tunic Ornament

## 19. Tunic Fragment with Clavus Section

*Colors and design:* The clavus band is bordered with a spiral-wave pattern and filled with lozenges, solid lozenges alternating with outlined ones. At one point, the band is interrupted by a rectangle containing a motif representing a dolphin. The band terminates with a pendant leaf on a long stem. The design is entirely worked in purple. The ground is yellowish, perhaps the natural color of the wool discolored by time.

*Materials and construction:* This piece was woven entirely of wool. The basic weave is tabby, 13 x 13. The tapestry insert was woven on grouped warps. From the reverse side of the piece it is evident that the spiral border was woven as a series of lopsided scallops. "Stitches" in the center of the upper parts of the scallops produce the effect of a spiral-wave motif. (These are not actually stitches in the true sense, but extensions of the background weave.) The dots in the ground are connected by long weft floats. Short, self-colored bands were formed in the weft by putting a weft bundle partway through the shed and then returning it in the counter-shed. About 5 cm of three of these bands are extant.

*Dimensions:* 15.8 x 38 cm.

*Date:* Fifth century.

*Accession number:* 389-2418.

*Remarks:* Dolphins, believed by ancient and some modern peoples to save humans from drowning, are symbols of salvation in several religions. In ancient times, dolphins were thought to be fish. A depiction of a fish was frequently used to symbolize Christ because in Greek, the word for fish, ἸΧΘΥ῾Σ, can be read as an acrostic for a sentence that translated means "Jesus Christ Son of God Savior." The dolphin-fish motif could have been worn by both pagans and Christians for much the same purpose, protection.

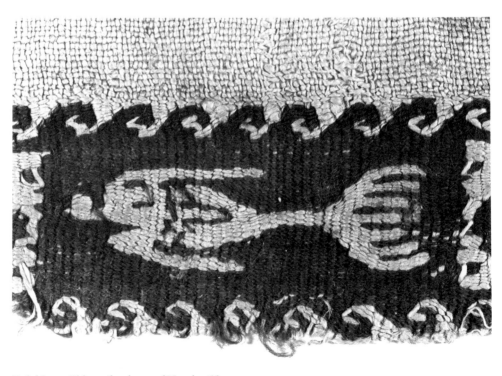

*Dolphin motif from the clavus of Number 19*

19. *Tunic Fragment with Clavus Section*   ↔

## 20. Tunic Fragment

*Colors and design:* The design areas on this fragment are a rectangular motif from the shoulder portion of the tunic and a part of one clavus. The rectangle has a spiral-wave border. Inside is an oval framing an armed man, perhaps a gladiator. The clavus is decorated with a well-formed stylized grapevine with leaves and grape clusters. Level with the shoulder motif is a small, equal-armed, dark purple cross with dots in the angles. A second cross, this one light on dark appears in a small rectangle at one end of the clavus. The design was executed in linen and wool yarns. The latter is now dark purple tinged with brown, but the color may have been brighter originally.

*Materials and construction:* The ground is natural linen rep, 20 x 13. The clavus and the shoulder rectangle are tapestry, woven on grouped warps in wool and linen yarns. The rep ground has *shadow* weft stripes formed of bundles of weft. The shots forming the stripes occur in pairs or in groups of three. Tapestry ornaments have curved wefts that follow the lines of the design. Small details were picked out in linen yarn worked as erratic weft floats while weaving was in progress.

*Dimensions:* 15 x 34 cm. Rectangular shoulder ornament, 8 x 5.8 cm. Width of clavus, 1.5 cm.

*Date:* Fifth century.

*Accession number:* 389-2379.

*Remarks:* While the decorative motifs on this fragment are Classical in origin, the crosses may indicate that the original owner of the tunic was a Christian or someone who believed that the cross served as a protective device. The fully dressed and armed warrior is set to fight mortal dangers, not spiritual ones, yet may also have a protective intent. The size of the decorative elements indicates that the tunic was a small one, no doubt intended for a child.

20. Tunic Fragment

*Warrior figure in inset decorating Number 20*

## 21. Fragment of a Textile Ornament

*Colors and design:* The fragment retains a group of figures rendered in dark brown on a linen ground that is considerably discolored. The design is a roundel delineated by a plain, solid-color band enclosing a group of men and lions. The men are armed with large stones and small shields, and they wear short mantles. Each attacks a lion. The lion-man groups face in opposite directions and are set one above the other on a diagonal.

*Materials and construction:* What remains of the piece is tapestry on grouped linen warps, linen and wool weft, 15 x 40. Curving wefts help to accentuate the design. A few small details appear to be embroidered.

*Dimensions:* 9.5 x 8 cm.

*Related examples:* The style and form of ornamentation on a child's tunic in Brooklyn, acc. # 749 (Thompson 1971:44, no. 17) is quite similar to the Rietz fragment.

*Date:* Late fifth or early sixth century.

*Accession number:* 389-2383.

*Remarks:* The appearance of the textile of which this is a fragment may be inferred from the Brooklyn child's tunic. In the Brooklyn example, the roundel (really more nearly an oval) that contains the figures is set in a rectangle that is in turn framed with a rinceau. Battles between men and animals are thought to signify the struggle between the good and evil in human nature. The idea is an ancient one, retained in later times.

*21. Fragment of a Textile Ornament*

## 22. Tunic Fragment with Insert Roundel

*Colors and design:* The roundel has a border of triangles and contains the motif of a lion cub along with leafy-spray filler motifs. The design elements were worked in purple on an ecru ground.

*Materials and construction:* The ground is linen in a near-tabby weave, 22 x 19. The insert is wool and linen tapestry with weft float details.

*Dimensions:* 14 x 14 cm.

*Date:* Fifth century.

*Accession number:* 389-2431.

*Remarks:* As mentioned in the remarks for Number 14, single lion motifs may have a protective purpose.

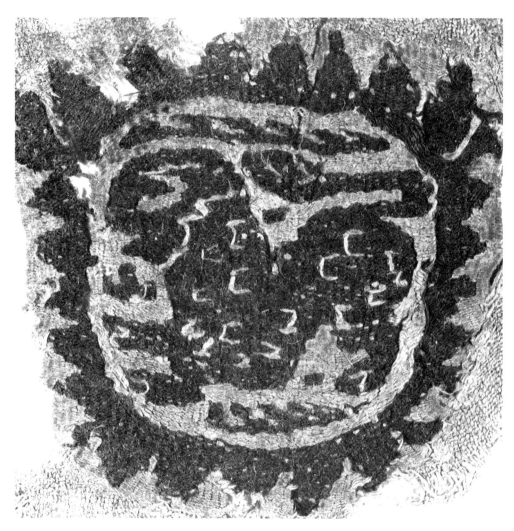

*22. Tunic Fragment with Insert Roundel*

## 23. Fragment of a Square Tunic Ornament

*Colors and design:* The brown pattern elements that decorate this fragment have a beige, originally white, ground. The motif is square, and it is bordered with small roundels, "pearls," seven on a side. A large roundel in the center contains a depiction of a running hound surrounded by leafy sprays.

*Materials and construction:* Most of what remains of this fragment was woven in tapestry on grouped linen warps, wool and linen weft, 6 x 24-48, and rep, all linen, 16 x 14. Normal tapestry technique with weft shots curved to accentuate lines of design.

*Dimensions:* 10.5 x 11 cm.

*Date:* Fifth century.

*Accession number:* 389-2387.

*Remarks:* The "pearl" border of this piece is a common design feature of Persian silks. In Eastern art, jewelled frames imply that the subject so decorated is special in some way—magical or spiritual.

## 24. Pair of Tunic Sleeve Ornaments

*Colors and design:* Each sleeve ornament consists of two nearly identical bands, with brownish purple figures and borders on a tan, originally white, ground. The same design elements occur on both sleeves. Each band has inverted arcade borders and crenellated ends. At the upper end of three of the bands is a nude warrior carrying a shield, at the lower another nude warrior wearing a sword-belt and holding the left hand aloft. The same warriors appear on the fourth band, but their positions are reversed. Between the two warriors, and placed at a right angle to their line of march, is a small running lion. Dots act as filler motifs.

*Materials and construction:* The foundation is linen rep, 16 x 12; the ornamentation is tapestry, wool and linen on linen warp, 8 x 36, with weft-float details. Normal tapestry technique was used with a minimal use of weft floats. The tapestry elements are whip-stitched to the rep textile pieces, an indication that the pieces were originally part of another garment.

*Dimensions:* a, 22 x 30; b, 22 x 26 cm.

*Date:* Sixth century.

*Accession number:* 389-2408 A-B.

*Remarks:* See remarks for Number 16, which has some of the same motifs but which is earlier in style. The raised hand is an ancient gesture of blessing or protection.

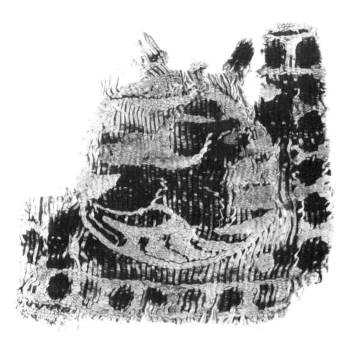

23. *Fragment of a Square Tunic Ornament*

24. *Pair of Tunic Sleeve Ornaments*  ↔  ↔

## 25. Fragment of a Tunic Sleeve

*(Color plate, page 70)*

*Colors and design:* The fragment has a dark yellow ground with figures and borders in dark brown. The design is a band with spiral-wave borders framing a row of figures. The figures that remain on the fragment are two warriors and, between them, a small lion. The ground line along which the lion runs is at a right angle to that of the warriors.

*Materials and construction:* The entire piece is woven in tapestry, wool weft on wool warp, 8 x 20–50. The weaving is fine and even and the reverse is unusually neat with short weft floats.

*Dimensions:* 7.6 x 20.3 cm.

*Date:* A ninth- or tenth-century version of a sixth-century motif.

*Accession number:* 389-2381.

*Remarks:* The yellow ground and certain features of the design indicate that the piece may have been made during a period of persecution after the Arab conquest when Coptic Egyptians were required to wear yellow garments, either during the time of the Tulunid governors, 868–906, or the succeeding Ikhshidid dynasty, 935–969. The piece is another member of the class of Coptic textiles discussed in the remarks for Number 16.

---

## 26. Tunic Ornament

*Colors and design:* An ovoid medallion forms the base for the ornament. In the center is a depiction of an eagle with outspread wings, dull purple on a tan ground. It is surrounded by a wide purple border. Within this is a narrower band with a net-pattern filler.

*Materials and construction:* The weave is tapestry, wool and linen wefts on paired linen warps, 9 x 22. Weft floats define details of the plumage and the intricate pattern of the border.

*Dimensions:* 11 x 13 cm.

*Related examples:* A larger fragment with a similar medallion is in Washington D.C., Textile Museum 71.128 (Trilling 1982, no. 40). It includes a section of the clavus, decorated with a net pattern that matches the border of the medallion.

*Date:* Fifth or early sixth century.

*Accession number:* 389-2587.

*Remarks:* The eagle as a symbol has an important place in several religions. The Roman legions marched under a standard bearing the image of an eagle. For Christians, it is the symbol of Saint John the Evangelist.

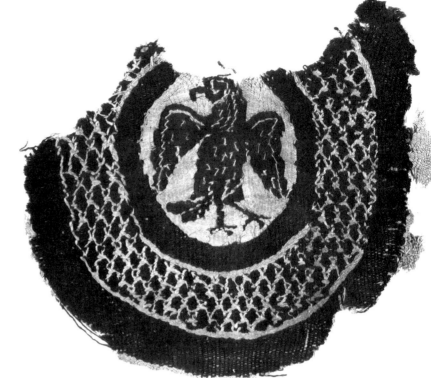

26. Tunic Ornament

25. Fragment of a Tunic Sleeve   ↔

By the sixth century two basic types of textile ornaments were used to decorate garments. One, which was in use before the fourth century, was essentially monochrome. Designs in the monochrome class were both non-representational and figurative—the latter included a wide range of subject matter: plant, animal, human, and mythological. The second type is polychrome. Polychrome textiles had been made earlier, but not for use as garments. Extant examples are thought to have been decorative hangings, woven pictures as it were, that are commonly called tapestries. The use of what are essentially miniature tapestries for embellishing clothing is believed to have begun in the sixth century and to have lasted well into the Muslim period.

## 27. Square Tunic Ornament

*Colors and design:* The reddish brown ornamentation has a tan ground. The design is organized as a circle contained in a square, the corners filled with simple plant motifs. In the center is a wide-eyed running warrior carrying a shield.

*Materials and construction:* The foundation is linen tabby, 15 x 15; the decoration is wool and linen tapestry on grouped linen warps, 10 x 52. The square ornament was cut from another garment, the edges turned under and whip-stitched to the tabby foundation.

*Dimensions:* 9 x 9 cm.

*Date:* Sixth century.

*Accession number:* 389-2430.

*Remarks:* This piece may have been cut from a larger textile ornament with a number of figures contained in a rinceau. The drawing is too sketchy to be certain, but the warrior appears to be nude, hence, a warrior of the spirit rather than of the flesh. His antagonist may have occupied an adjacent compartment in the rinceau.

## 28. Fragment of a Tapestry Square from a Cushion(?)

*Colors and design:* This fragment is part of a square motif with a wide, compound border enclosing five roundels, a small one in each corner, a large one in the center. The pattern is worked in purple, green, orange, and red on a cream-colored ground. The main part of the border contains a braid delineated in white on a purple ground. At the outer edge is an inverted arcade with a small roundel under each arch. What remains of the large central roundel indicates that it may have contained a representation of a centaur. The one extant corner roundel contains a male figure wearing a short cloak and apparently trampling grapes, represented by thirteen purple dots. Next to this corner roundel is a vase from which grows a grapevine.

*Materials and construction:* The piece was woven entirely in tapestry with wool and linen weft on wool warp, 11 x 40. Details and the pattern of the border were worked in weft floats.

*Dimensions:* 9 x 14.5 cm.

*Date:* Sixth century.

*Accession number:* 389-2385

*Remarks:* The 3.4 cm of surviving selvedge indicates that the piece may have been woven as a single unit that was then stitched to a larger textile. Similar specimens have been discovered attached to weft-loop-pile textiles intended to cover cushions. This piece belongs to a large group of polychrome textiles that retain design elements derived from Greek art but which have acquired

27. *Square Tunic Ornament*

28. *Fragment of a Tapestry Square from a Cushion(?)*

Christian symbolism. Vintage scenes showing the crushing of the grapes to make wine can be understood as a symbol for the sacrifice of Jesus. An overflowing vase, here overflowing with grapevines, sometimes signifies one of the rivers of Paradise. When complete, the design may have included a total of four vases, one for each of the four rivers of Paradise. A centaur or a horseman is a symbol of good, controlling or attempting to control one's baser instincts. Colorful as this piece is, it should be noted that the disposition of the colors is not at all realistic. Purple is the dominant color, used for the border, the rinceau, and the figures, while red, green, and orange enliven the minor details.

## 29. Two Square Garment Ornaments

*Colors and design:* The ground is ecru and the design elements are purple with touches of crimson. In the center of each square is a smaller square of solid purple. This is bordered by an inhabited rinceau, the tendrils forming roundels. Each of these contains either a lion wearing a red collar or a hound with red ribbons streaming from its neck. Interstices are filled with small floral motifs.

*Materials and construction:* The ground is linen near-tabby, 25 x 22, and the ornamentation is wool and linen tapestry woven on grouped linen warps, 10 x 80. From the reverse of the better-preserved square it can be seen that the tapestry section was woven on a limited number of the available warps, the unused ones left to float at the back of the tapestry portion. The tapestry was woven with weft that was separate from that of the tabby ground. The unwoven tabby weft was allowed to float behind the unused warp, making two layers of floats and one layer of tapestry, three layers in all.

*Dimensions:* 12.4 x 7.5 cm.

*Date:* Sixth or early seventh century.

*Accession number:* 389-2433.

*Remarks:* The streamers worn by the hounds reflect Persian influence. They are thought to indicate that the wearers possessed supernatural or other special attributes. Collars on animals—in this example, lions— have a different meaning; they represent control of the wilder aspects of animal nature.

*29a. and 29b. Two Square Garment Ornaments*

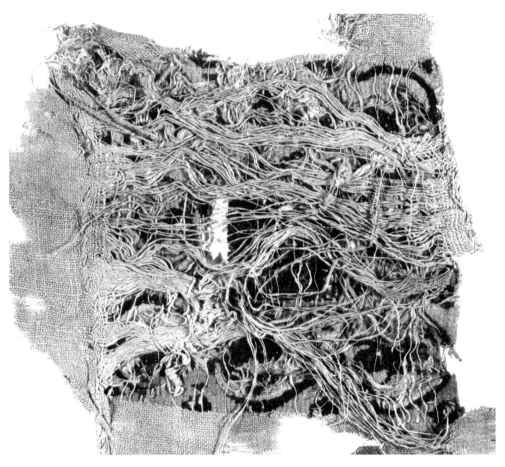

*Back of Number 29 b., showing unused warps and wefts*

## 30. Fragment of a Decorated Textile

*Colors and design:* The framework of the design is a simple rinceau. In the roundels formed by the stems are a kneeling man, a basket, and a large-eyed hound wearing a broad collar. Vine and figures are purple with touches of yellow, and the basket is red, yellow, and green. The background is cream.

*Materials and construction:* What remains of the textile is tapestry weave, wool and linen wefts on paired linen warps, 7 x 14. The weft shots follow the curves of the design rather than crossing in straight lines. The warps are strictly divided, two by two.

*Dimensions:* 28 x 8 cm.

*Date:* Early sixth century.

*Accession number:* 389-2378.

*Remarks:* Like Number 28, this fragment may have been a part of a square cushion ornament. For the symbolism of the dog wearing a collar see remarks the for Number 29.

---

## 31. Tunic Fragments, Yoke and Shoulder Ornaments

*(Additional illustrations on pages 122 – 123)*

*Colors and design:* The pieces are extremely discolored. The original color scheme was undoubtedly white with purple figures accented in red. The purple has now turned dark brown. From the remains it can be determined that the tunic had a deep yoke with several horizontal bands. The principal band holds an arcade, really a series of *aediculae*, each occupied by a dancer, nude except for a floating scarf worn over the shoulders. Two bands above this contain lozenges, the band below it, a chain of trefoils. On either side of the yoke were clavi of which but one now remains. These contained two sizes of linked cartouches, the larger enclosing dancers similar to those in the yoke arcade, the smaller, busts. A second fragment of the same tunic has the remains of a square that may be from the shoulder area. It bears a geometric pattern of lozenges.

*Materials and construction:* The technique used is tapestry in wool and linen on paired linen warps. Open slits in the uppermost yoke band enhance the decorative effect of the ornamentation.

*Dimensions:* Yoke fragment, 40 x 48 cm, shoulder fragment, 10 x 11 cm.

*Related example:* Paris, Louvre, inv. 4307 (Du Bourguet 1964, no. C 32).

*Date:* Sixth century.

*Accession number:* 389-2539.

*Remarks:* Nude dancers as decorative motifs are a common feature of Coptic textiles, persisting even after the Muslim conquest. Nudity symbolizes spiritual purity when it appears in a religious context as may be the case here, indicated by the placement of the figures in an architectural context that suggests a side aisle of a church nave.

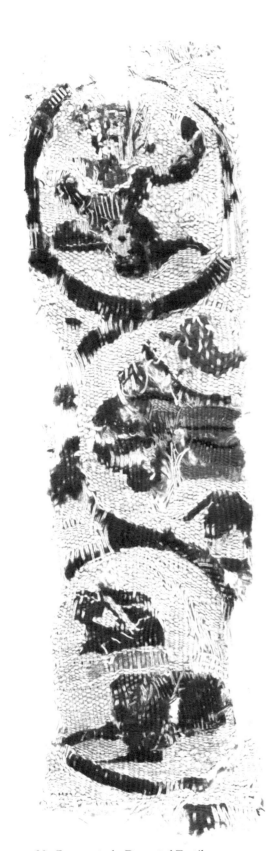

30. *Fragment of a Decorated Textile*

*Dancer on clavus of Number 31*  ↔

*31. Tunic Fragment*   ↔

*Dancer in aedicula on yoke band of Number 31* ↔

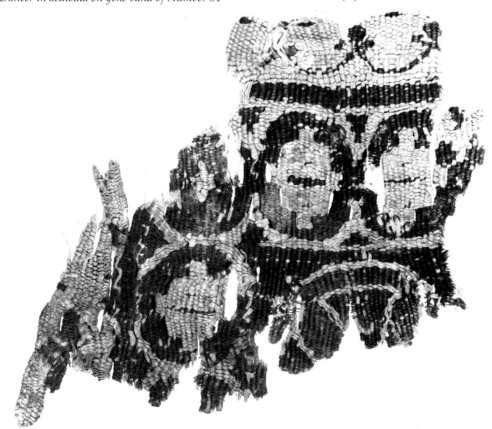

*Fragment of Shoulder(?) Inset of Number 31*

## 32. Fragments of Tunic Clavi

*Colors and design:* The design is worked in brownish purple on a beige ground. The band has spiral-wave edge borders enclosing motifs of warriors and lions. The warriors hold their right hands in the air. The lions are positioned at right angles to the ground lines of the warriors.

*Materials and construction:* The piece was woven in tapestry with wool warp and weft, 7 x 40. The details are worked in weft floats. There are some grouped wefts in the ground.

*Dimensions:* 8 x 14 cm.

*Date:* The specimen is a late example of a common sixth-century design. It may be ninth century in date.

*Accession number:* 389-2412

*Remarks:* The two fragments belong to the same garment but are not contiguous.

## 33. A Pair of Fragmentary Sleeves with Decorated Inserts

*(Illustrated on pages 126 – 127)*

*Colors and design:* The decorative motifs are worked in brown on a tan ground. The organization of the design of each sleeve forms a rectangle consisting of two bands with borders of reversed scallops. Each band is divided into two sections, each section containing depictions of a pair of worshippers(?) inside of an Ionic building with a decorated pediment. At least three of the pediments contain female busts, possibly of goddesses. A second pair of figures floats vaporlike in the air above the roof. The peak of the roof is ornamented with a palmate acroterion. All of the full-length figures have one hand raised, and the ones at ground level are depicted with crossed legs.

*Materials and construction:* The technique is tapestry, woven entirely in wool, 10 x 28–34. The selvedges were woven with extra warps, for reinforcement.

*Dimensions:* 22 x 29 cm and 28 x 25 cm.

*Related examples:* Two similarly decorated textiles are in Moscow, Pushkin Museum inv. #6962 and 610 (Shurinova 1967, no. 137, 168).

*Date:* Eighth century or later.

*Accession numbers:* 389-2451 and 389-2452.

*Remarks:* There are several possible interpretations of the subject matter used to ornament these sleeves. Figures with crossed legs are fairly common in Coptic textiles: the position is believed to indicate the activity of dancing. A Gnostic text, the *Acts of John*, tells how the disciples under the direction of Jesus danced with him the night before his arrest (Pagels 1981:89). The purpose of this dance was to make the individual one with Christ. It is therefore probable that the representations of dancers, both male and female, referred to such a belief. In this example there is, in addition to the dancers, a sense of dualism conveyed by the many pairs of beings and buildings in the design. Manichaeanism, which in Egypt merged with Gnosticism in the later Coptic period, stressed dualism, and may have been the religion of the wearer for whom the garment was woven.

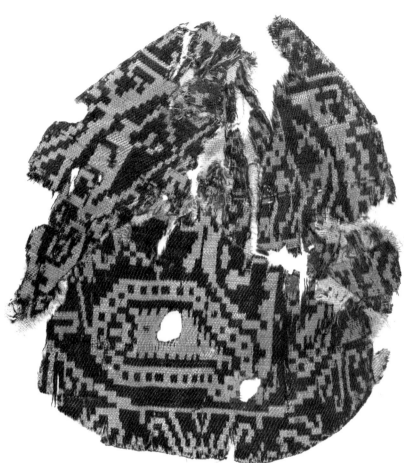

34. *Tunic Shoulder-Band Pendant Medallion from Akhmîm*  ↔

32. *Fragments of a Tunic Clavi*

*33 a. One of a Pair of Fragmentary Sleeves with Decorated Inserts*  ↔

*Looms and Textiles of the Copts*

*Detail of Number 33 a., showing buildings with worshippers inside and floating spirits above the roofs* ↔

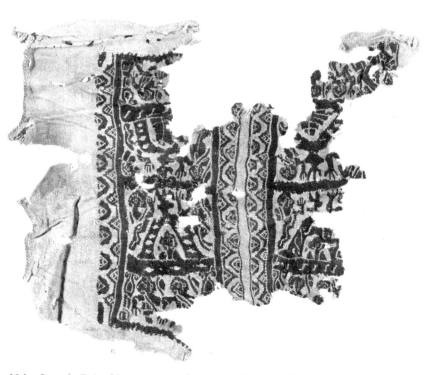

*33 b. One of a Pair of Fragmentary Sleeves with Decorated Inserts* ↔

## 34. Tunic Shoulder-Band Pendant Medallion from Akhmîm

*(Illustrated on page 125)*

*Colors and design:* Cream-colored warp, light green and cream-colored weft. Symmetrical floral design composed of small block-shaped units. The back of the textile shows the design in reverse.

*Materials and construction:* A silk, weft-face drawloom twill, there is one main warp between two binder warps with three main warps to a pattern unit. The warp is single-ply Z-twist; the weft yarns appear to have no twist at all. The piece is heavily damaged and has been crudely and wrongly restored by pasting small pieces of linen cloth to the back. Its original form can be conjectured by the observation of related textiles in other collections. Edges of the piece have been folded under, indicating that it was appliquéd to a garment.

*Dimensions:* 11 x 12 cm.

*Related examples:* London, Victoria and Albert Museum, 798, 799 (Kendrick 1922); Textile Museum, Washington D.C., 721.10 (Bellinger 1950–52:15).

*Date:* Fifth century in style, but perhaps later in construction.

*Accession number:* 389-2386.

*Remarks:* A linen garment with silk appliqués woven in a similar style is extant, London, Victoria and Albert Museum, 794 (Kendrick 1922). Drawloom textiles of the class to which the Rietz specimen belongs had a long life (see Grube 1962). The complexity of the weave was such that it discouraged creativity or even experimentation with modest variations, so once drafted, a pattern tended to remain unchanged for generations. Akhmîm is the modern name for the ancient city of Panopolis. It may have been a center for the production of drawloom silks. In the Early Christian period a large monastery was founded nearby, the White Monastery, which still stands and is used as a place of worship.

## 35. Two Fragments of a Tunic from Assyūt

*(Color plate, page 71)*

*Colors and design:* One fragment is from a sleeve of the tunic and it is ornamented with a polychrome design organized in bands on a beige ground. The lower two bands are decorated with a pink-and-green lozenge pattern with Greek crosses as filler motifs. These have yellow and green borders of spiral-wave design. The upper band contains two rows of dark blue and light green flying genii wearing derbylike hats and carrying large bowls in their out-stretched arms. The other fragment is from the yoke. This fragment contains three figured bands separated by rows of geometric motifs resembling spearheads and hooks in shades of yellow, green, and pink. The upper two figured bands contain pink and dark blue running hounds, each in a cartouche. The lower band contains green creatures with long snouts, crocodiles(?).

*Materials and construction:* The technique of both pieces is tapestry, wool and linen weft on two-ply Z-twist linen warps. The thread count of the sleeve piece is 5 x 54, of the yoke piece, 6 x 50. Portions of both side selvedges are preserved on the sleeve fragment.

*Dimensions:* sleeve pieces, 23 x 27.5 cm and yoke piece, 23 x 21 cm.

*Date:* Seventh century.

*Accession numbers:* 389-2400 and 389-2404.

*Remarks:* Assyūt, the presumed provenance of this piece, may not have been its place of manufacture. The figure style of the textile places it in a class of textiles produced in a weaving center believed to have been located farther south, in Upper Egypt.

*35 a. Sleeve Fragment of Tunic from Assyūt*

*35 b. Yoke Fragment of Tunic from Assyūt*

## 36. Square Decorative Garment Insert

(Color plate, page 72)

*Colors and design:* The ground of the square is dark blue, with a border of red hooks. The center motif of four birds seated in a fanciful, symmetrical plant, is worked in pink, green, and off-white.

*Materials and construction:* The weave is tapestry, wool warp, linen and wool weft, 14–16 x 27.

*Dimensions:* 7 x 6.4 cm.

*Related examples:* Washington D.C., Textile Museum (Riefstahl 1941, no. 178).

*Date:* Sixth century.

*Accession number:* 389-2388.

*Remarks:* Essentially, this is a tree-of-life motif in abbreviated form. The motif refers to a tree in the garden of Eden and also to the Tree, that is the cross, of the Crucifixion. (The connection between this cross and the tree of life is sometimes indicated by placing birds in the angles made by the cross arm, as can be seen in another textile in the Rietz Collection, Number 37.) Different varieties of birds have particular meanings in Early Christian art. Doves, perhaps the smaller of the two birds depicted here, signify deliverance and the Holy Ghost. Peacocks, the two larger birds, are symbols of immortality. The tree-of-life motif is fairly common in Coptic textiles, usually rendered in a style related to that of Sassanian silks.

## 37. Fragment of an Ecclesiastical Tapestry from Bawit(?)

(Color plate, page 73)

*Colors and design:* The elements of the design were worked in two shades of dull yellow, a brick red, dull green, and indigo blue. What remains of the design is a portion of a decorated band framed by two narrower plain ones. In the center of the main band is a strangely formed quadruped with hooves, large ears, and a long, thick tail. On the right is a jeweled cross with four birds in the angles formed by the upright and crossbar. On the left is an unoccupied jeweled throne, only partly preserved, with a bird above the remaining arm. Four small beasts with long ears and tails fill the remaining areas of the background.

*Materials and construction:* The fragment was woven in tapestry weave, entirely in wool, 9 x 20. It was carefully worked; the back of the piece appears nearly the same as the front, with no hanging threads and almost no weft floats.

*Dimensions:* 12.4 x 17.5 cm.

*Related examples:* Jeweled crosses with birds in the angles appear on textiles in London, Victoria and Albert Museum (Kendrick 1921: no. 313 pl. 5, no. 314 pl. 6).

*Date:* Sixth century.

*Accession number:* 389-2380.

*Remarks:* The themes on this textile fragment are decidedly Christian in nature and are often found in Byzantine art. The empty throne symbolizes the preparation for the second coming of Christ. The jeweled cross signifies the Transfiguration of Christ. The beast may represent one of the Evangelists, Saint Luke, in his symbolic form of a bull. If so, the other three Evangelists were undoubtedly also present on the tapestry when it was complete. The theme of the vacant jeweled throne, the *Hetoimasia*, appears in the cupola mosaics of the Arian Baptistery in Ravenna, built in the late fifth century (Paolucci 1978:55). The Rietz tapestry is slightly later in date. Since it was woven with both sides nearly alike, the piece may have belonged to a church or baptistery door curtain. Bawit, where the piece is thought to have been found, is the site of a large and important monastery that grew and flourished for nearly a millenium. It was founded by a follower of Saint Pachomius the Great in the early fifth century. A large burial ground associated with it has been a rich source of textile remains.

36. *Square Decorative Garment Insert*

37. *Fragment of an Ecclesiastical Tapestry from Bawit(?)*

## 38. Composite Textile Fragment

*Colors and design:* The foundation textile is red brown and ornamented with a large roundel flanked by two smaller ones, medium red in color, one containing a Greek cross in a circle, the other an eight-petaled rosette, both worked in dark yellow. The large roundel has a yellow ground and originally may have contained the motif of a peacock with outspread tail. A circle was cut out of the center of this roundel, leaving a yellow band and the "eyes" of the peacock's tailfeathers. The band encloses two figures wearing halos worked in white, black, light green, and yellow on a pink ground.

*Materials and construction:* The weave is linen and wool tapestry on linen warp, some of it dyed, 9 x 32. This textile is actually made up of parts from two or three textiles trimed to shape and pasted together. The warp of the figured portion runs at right angles to the warp of the foundation textile and is of a different color.

*Dimensions:* 13.7 x 21 cm.

*Date:* Sixth century (?)

*Accession number:* 389-2429.

*Remarks:* At first glance this pastiche appears to show a depiction of Christ and a disciple. The piece is a model example of the pitfalls that await collectors who fail to inspect textile specimens through a magnifying glass, examining both sides and paying special attention to repairs that may disguise the addition of unrelated material.

## 39. Garment Ornament

*(Illustrated on page 135)*

*Colors and design:* The form is a roundel with a double border ornamented with a rope pattern. In the center is a half-length figure of a crowned, nimbate woman with dark, wavy hair and elaborate earrings. One hand, holding an object of uncertain identity, is upraised. Colors are tan, black, cream, dark yellow, dull red, and dull medium green.

*Materials and construction:* The piece is tapestry, wool and linen weft on linen warp. The latter is two-ply Z-twist. The count is 11 x 48.

*Dimensions:* 7.4 x 8 cm.

*Date:* Late sixth or early seventh century.

*Accession number:* 389-2585.

*Remarks:* Women with halos are common in Coptic art. This example may represent Isis, or a Christian saint, perhaps Mary Magdalene, a popular figure for Copts because of her later life spent as a hermit. Coptic Christians consider living a life devoted to religious practices, apart and alone, to be particularly meritorious.

*38. Composite Textile Fragment*

## 40. Garment Ornament

*(Color plate, page 74)*

*Colors and design:* The form is a roundel. In the center is a representation of a mermaid holding a conch shell and being accompanied by a fish. The border is a stair-step jewel inlay design. The colors are light brown, cream, black, dark yellow, dull red, dull light green, and dull medium green.

*Materials and construction:* The weave is tapestry, wool and linen weft on two-ply Z-twist linen warp.

*Dimensions:* 8 x 7 cm.

*Date:* Sixth or seventh century.

*Accession number:* 389-2584.

*Remarks:* Representations of mermaids have a long history in ancient Mediterranean and Near Eastern art. As symbols of belief, their significance is not clear, especially in Christian contexts. The stair-step border design is not particularly suitable for a woven roundel and may be derived from another form of art entirely. Stair-step inlays occur in gold and garnet jewelry of the fifth and sixth centuries, a fact that suggests a metalwork source for the motif.

*40. Garment Ornament*

39. *Garment Ornament* ↔

After the Arab conquest in the mid-seventh century, Coptic textile design changed its character, moving ever more distant from its classical Roman and Greek sources. In part, this was a reaction against the Byzantine culture, associated in the Coptic mind with oppression. Contributing to the change may have been Islamic prohibitions against depicting human and animal figures. Such figures when they appear in Coptic textiles of the later periods become increasingly abstract to the point of being virtually unrecognizable.

## 41. Fragment of a Tunic Clavus

*Colors and design:* What remains is a multi-colored band with double jewel inlay borders framing a variety of motifs: two nude dancers, a winged child, a winged dog, and a fragmentary motif that may represent the lower part of a standing, robed figure. On a dark pink ground, figures and borders are worked in medium pink, black, light green, gray, beige, and dull yellow.

*Materials and construction:* The fragment is tapestry, woven with wool and linen weft, linen warp, 8 x 36.

*Dimensions:* 9 x 11 cm.

*Date:* Seventh century.

*Accession number:* 389-2390.

*Remarks:* This clavus fragment is mounted on a linen cloth, perhaps ancient, but unrelated. Turned-under edges indicate that the piece was reused in antiquity. The theme of the motif could be Dionysian, the robed figure representing this god.

## 42. Rectangle Cut from the Upper Part of a Tunic

*(Additional illustrations on pages 138 – 139)*

*Colors and design:* The clavi bands have semicircular ends and borders of jewel inlay with epsilon-shaped cells. Each band is ornamented with a haloed figure wearing an elaborate robe and carrying a lyre. The space remaining is occupied by four symmetrical plant motifs. The tapestry bands are worked in dark yellow, dull red, dark blue, light green, and tan. The plain foundation textile is a brownish yellow.

*Materials and construction:* The weave of both the ground and the clavi is tapestry, wool warp and weft, 8–10 x 34. The clavi are whip-stitched to the plain tapestry textile.

*Dimensions:* 35 x 46 cm.

*Related examples:* Figures depicted in the same style appear on a piece in Washington, D. C., Textile Museum (Riefstahl 1941:257). See also Kybelova (1967:130, pl. 86).

*Date:* Seventh century.

*Accession number:* 389-2409.

*Remarks:* From this point onward the human figure becomes increasingly stylized, moving farther and farther away from Greek anatomical canons.

41. *Fragment of a Tunic Clavus*

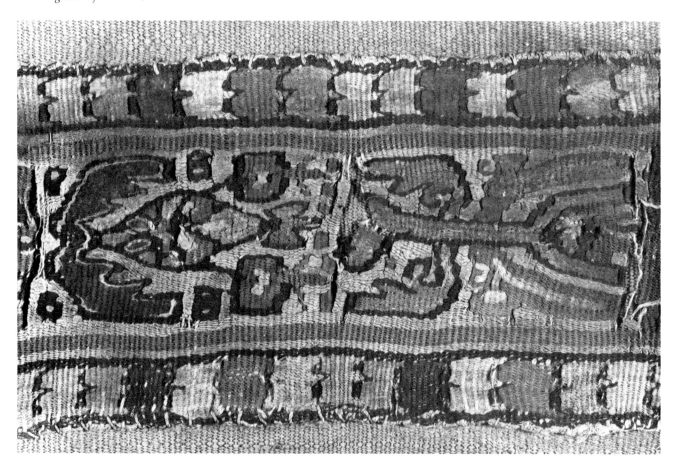

*Plant motifs from the clavus of Number 42*

*Robed figure holding lyre(?) from clavus of Number 42*

42. *Rectangle Cut from the Upper Part of a Tunic*

↔

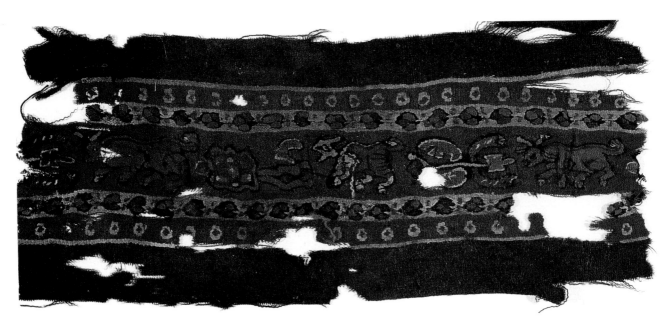

44. *Section Cut from a Banded Textile* (*See catalog entry, page 148*)

52. *Tunic Sleeve Fragment* *(See catalog entry, page 158)*   ↔

64. *Fragment of a Curtain with a False Kufic Inscription  (See catalog entry, page 172)*  ↔

65. *Fragment of a Tunic* *(See catalog entry, page 172)*

↔

*66. Square Tunic Ornament  (See catalog entry, page 176)*

67. *Section of a Tunic Sleeve  (See catalog entry, page 176)*

*43. Part of a Coverlet or Hanging from Bawit(?)*

## 43. Part of a Coverlet or Hanging from Bawit(?)

*Colors and design:* The allover design is composed of plain bands alternating with figured ones. The figured bands have compound borders consisting of a plain band and one occupied by trefoils linked by half-circles. Fabulous beings and symmetrical plant forms comprise the motifs of the figured bands. The ground is dark pink, and the dividing borders and figures are worked in dull red, beige, medium pink, blue-green, and black.

*Materials and construction:* The weave is tapestry, worked entirely in wool, 7 x 38. The warp has been dyed.

*Dimensions:* 26 x 17.5 cm.

*Date:* Seventh century.

*Accession number:* 389-2399.

*Remarks:* The fanciful nature of the figures, the trefoil borders, and the general organization of the design all recall the much earlier banded embroidered textile found in Noin Ula, which has Hellenistic elements in its design (Trever l932, pl. 3, 7). For notes on the presumed find site of the Rietz textile see the remarks for Number 37.

*Detail of Number 43 showing two fabulous beings*

## 44. Section Cut from a Banded Textile

*(Color plate, page 140)*

*Colors and design:* The design scheme consists of a decorated red band between two plain dark-blue ones. The red band has double borders, the outer border ornamented with tan Greek crosses, the inner border with linked tricolor ivy leaves on a tan ground. The center of the band contains a procession of quadrupeds, some with horns. Between each animal is a formal plant motif. The animals and plants are worked in dull yellow, pink, light green, and medium green.

*Materials and construction:* The piece is tapestry, with wool warp and weft, 9 x 32.

*Dimensions:* 13.7 x 32 cm.

*Date:* Ninth or tenth century.

*Accession number:* 389-2415.

*Remarks:* Processions of animals have a long history in Classical art and derive from the Near East. This example represents an early Medieval version of the ancient theme.

*44. Section Cut from a Banded Textile*

## 45. Decorated Band Fragment

*Colors and design:* The piece has borders ornamented with motifs of fish. In one section the fish motif is interrupted by a rectangular panel containing six ovals. The latter may depict gems in broad settings. The middle of the band is filled with an allover pattern of symmetrical floral motifs. The ground is red; the jewels are green; and the design is worked in tan, blue-green, and black.

*Materials and construction:* The weave is tapestry, wool and linen weft on two-ply Z-twist warp, 10 x 66.

*Dimensions:* 8 x 33 cm.

*Date:* Tenth century.

*Accession number:* 389-2414.

*Remarks:* The fish may or may not symbolize Christ; their association with jewels suggests that their meaning has religious connotations. The tight placement of the motifs and the minimum of background are in marked contrast to earlier Coptic design habits and may be the result of Arabian influence.

*45. Decorated Band Fragment*

## 46. Tunic Clavus Fragment

*Colors and design:* The clavus has borders of dark gray and green triangles. Repeated down the center is a symmetrical floral motif woven in tan, light green, dark gray, yellow, light orange, and dark blue on a pink ground.

*Materials and construction:* Most of the piece was woven in tapestry, wool and linen weft on grouped linen warps, 8 x 30. Fragments of the surrounding linen textile have a count of 12 x 18.

*Dimensions:* 6 x 18 cm.

*Date:* Tenth century.

*Accession number:* 389-2436

*Remarks:* The highly stylized floral motif may refer to one of the trees of paradise. Motifs of this nature are thought to have Persian or Near Eastern origins.

## 47. Belt(?) Fragment

*Colors and design:* The design is organized as a continuous band with spiral-wave borders. The center is divided into alternate squares and rectangles, each containing an amoeba-like motif ornamented with X and O figures. Colors are yellow, red, medium green, and dark gray.

*Materials and construction:* The textile is a narrow tapestry weave with edge selvedges, one strongly reinforced with extra warp threads. The textile is made of wool and linen weft on linen warp, 9 x 39.

*Dimensions:* 20 x 6 cm.

*Date:* Tenth century.

*Accession number:* 389-2579.

*Remarks:* This piece would have been equally useful as a belt or as garment trimming. The one heavily reinforced edge would make the band suitable for edging a tunic neck. The design is, perhaps, derived from a floral motif of the type decorating the previous specimen, but considerably debased.

*46. Tunic Clavus Fragment*  ⟷  *47. Belt(?) Fragment*

## 48. Tunic Clavus Fragment

*Colors and design:* The clavus has a rounded end and a border of reverse arcade. The interior contains a three-part cartouche composed of a lozenge flanked by circles, all with folliage embellishment and a dwarf(?) enclosed in an oval frame of oak leaves and acorns. The clavus terminates in a short stem ending in an oval containing a cluster of three leaves. The design is carried out in brownish purple on a tan ground.

*Materials and construction:* Linen rep, 11 x 8; wool tapestry, 7 x 48. The rep foundation textile has *shadow* stripes made of pairs of bundled weft shots. Three shadow stripes lie under the clavus, a fourth lies directly alongside. The tapestry clavus was cut from another garment, the edges turned under and then stitched to the rep ground.

*Dimensions:* 13 x 42 cm.

*Date:* Seventh century or later.

*Accession number:* 389-2416.

*Remarks:* The decoration of the clavus is descended from the monochrome ornaments of the early period of Coptic weaving, but the quality of the design is closer to the early Medieval period. The monochrome textile ornament had a long life in Egypt. The human figure is nearly overwhelmed by the large scale of the surrounding foliage and the boldly outlined cartouches.

*Dwarf(?) from Clavus of Number 48*

48. *Tunic Clavus Fragment*　　↔　　49. *Mantle(?) Fragment*　　　　　　　　　↔

## 49. Mantle(?) Fragment

*(Illustrated on page 153)*

*Colors and design:* What remains of the garment is a band with dark yellow ground and brownish purple ornamentation. It has a compound border composed of a plain solid-color band edged with an outer band of two-pronged forks alternating with triple-dot clusters. The interior motifs consist of repeated units: an amphora from which grows a double vine with long, elaborate tendrils, which form enclosures for a mythical monster and a centaur. Each amphora sits on a rounded base decorated with a pair of fish and a pair of birds.

*Materials and construction:* The piece is tapestry, normal in weave, but exceptionally fine.

*Dimensions:* 12.5 x 28 cm.

*Date:* Seventh century or later.

*Accession number:* 389-2427.

*Remarks:* The design recalls Roman architectural plaster decoration. Like the previous example, the figures are subordinate to the geometric and floral motifs. The figures appear to have no special significance but are completely decorative in intent.

## 50. Fragment of a Tunic Sleeve

*Colors and design:* The sleeve is decorated with brown bands and figures on a cream-colored ground. The design is composed of two bands filled with figures and separated by a narrower band with a simple cable pattern. The outer border bands are edged with a reverse scallop, each point terminating with a vine leaf. (One border band is missing, but presumably it matched the other.) In the center of the figured bands are ovals, each containing the figure of a hare. Flanking the ovals are pairs of lozenges with vine scrolls at the corners, containing, respectively, a smaller lozenge with vine leaves, a pair of fish, a single fish, and a standing bird (a guineafowl?).

*Materials and construction:* The sleeve is tapestry, woven on paired warps with wool warp and weft, 16 x 24. There are many short slits left open.

*Dimensions:* 16 x 24 cm.

*Date:* Eighth century.

*Accession number:* 389-2392.

*Remarks:* The figured elements suggest a heraldic or a zodiacal symbolism with possible significance to the original owner of the textile.

50. *Fragment of a Tunic Sleeve*

## 51. Rectangle Cut from the Shoulder Area of a Tunic

*Colors and design:* Most of the piece is the natural color of undyed wool. The ornamentation, now in dark-brown yarn, may have been purple originally. Detached, linear cartouches interrupted by a rectangular panel containing the figure of a snake, light on a dark ground, compose the clavus decoration. The roundel has a spiral wave frame and contains the figure of a bird (a guineafowl?), with one leaf in its beak and another filling the space behind its head.

*Materials and construction:* The material is wool, woven in a near-tabby, 16–15 x 13–11, with tapestry inserts, 8 x 38. The tapestry roundel is set in a lentoid, a fact not immediately obvious because the points of the figure are woven in the same color and material as the main ground, but in tapestry, not tabby. The purpose of this was not decorative, but rather a means to avoid an abrupt transition between the ground and the insert that might weaken the textile.

*Dimensions:* 9 x 23 cm.

*Date:* Ninth century.

*Accession number:* 389-2423.

*Remarks:* The use of a lentoid as a technical, not a decorative, feature occurs on several other Rietz textiles and may be an indication of a particular weaver, workshop, or region. Serpents were important symbols in several first-millenium religions, often symbolizing wisdom. They had a special place in Gnosticism, in part due to the serpent in the Garden of Eden who instructed Eve.

*51. Rectangle Cut from the Shoulder Area of a Tunic*

*Detail of Number 51, showing the background around the inset, worked in tapestry weave of the same color as the ground.*

## 52. Tunic Sleeve Fragment

(Color plate, page 141)

*Colors and design:* The dark yellow ground is decorated with bands and figures in dull purple and dark green. The design is organized as two identical bands, each with a single line of reverse arcade on the outermost edge. The filler motif, a fish nibbling the stem of a floating water plant, is repeated nine times in each band. The motifs are disposed in double rows on each band, forming two processions of fish swimming in opposite directions.

*Materials and construction:* The weave is tapestry with wool warp and weft, 10 x 78.

*Dimensions:* 14 x 22 cm.

*Related example:* London, Victoria and Albert Museum (Kendrick 1920, no. 18 pl. 26; Baginski and Tidhar 1980:79, no. 97).

*Date:* Tenth century (?)

*Accession number:* 389-2391.

*Remarks:* The fish and water plant motif was a common one in ancient Egyptian art and continued in use during the Coptic period, one of the few ancient motifs to be retained by Coptic artists.

## 53. Tunic Sleeve Fragment

*Colors and design:* Originally there were two bands with similar ornamentation; now, only a ragged portion of one remains. The bands were divided by a strip of battlement meander. The outer edge of the extant band is decorated by a wave meander. The decorative motifs consist of guineafowl, plants, and fish(?) worked in medium brown on a beige ground.

*Materials and construction:* Woven entirely in wool, the part remaining is tapestry, with some doubled warps, 10 x 24. The warp yarn was dyed a dark yellow. It does not show in the extant fragment because of the closely packed weft yarns characteristic of the tapestry technique, but the use of colored warp implies that the body of the textile was woven in rep or tabby in weft dyed to match.

*Dimensions:* 10.7 x 26.4 cm.

*Date:* Tenth century.

*Accession number:* 389-2420.

*Remarks:* The yellow color postulated for the missing body of the tunic may indicate that this piece was woven during the Ikhshidid dynasty when Coptic Christians were required to wear yellow garments.

52. *Tunic Sleeve Fragment*

53. *Tunic Sleeve Fragment*

## 54. Section of a Tunic Neck Band(?)

*Colors and design:* The fragment is a polychrome band with one plain border and one jeweled border of rectangular "gems" in plain settings. The design motifs are flower sprays and a nude female dancer with a narrow, green scarf draped over her left arm and a basket or cornucopia of flowers held in her raised right hand. The figure and the borders are worked in beige, light green, and black on a dark rose-red ground.

*Materials and construction:* The band is woven in tapestry on linen warp with wool and linen weft, 10 x 58. One border is worked in such a manner as to give a three-dimensional effect, accomplished by overpacking the weft, thus causing the surface to pucker. There is a double row of twining on one end.

*Dimensions:* 5 x 18 cm.

*Date:* Ninth or tenth century.

*Accession number:* 389-2396.

*Remarks:* The piece was reused in antiquity. Nudity, as mentioned earlier, had connotations of purity. A tunic fragment in Brooklyn, Brooklyn Museum of Art acc. no. 38.753, is decorated with a nude woman dancing in an area defined by a representation of a chain supporting a jeweled cross (Thompson 1971:82-83).

## 55. Upper Portion of a Tunic Front

*(Additional illustration on page 163)*

*Colors and design:* The polychrome design on a dark pink ground is organized as a rectangular panel framed on three sides by plain and figured dark blue bands. Some of the figures appear to represent butterflies: the others are nude dancers. At the upper end of the panel is a rectangle containing stylized figures that could represent satyrs and maenads. Standing in the center is an imposing, robed figure.

*Materials and construction:* The technique is tapestry, 7 x 30, woven entirely in wool and so carefully worked that the front and the back are nearly identical.

*Dimensions:* 39 x 27 cm.

*54. Section of a Tunic Neck Band(?)*

55. *Upper Portion of a Tunic Front* ↔

*Date:* Tenth century.

*Accession number:* 389-2405.

*Remarks:* The figure in the center may be Dionysus or Orpheus. Some late antique religious cults worshipped Dionysus or Orpheus in connection with Neopythagoreanism, interpreting them as representations of sacrifice and rebirth. The figures in the border, butterflies and putti, are emblems of Eros and Psyche, mythical figures whose story was given meaning on a metaphysical level by certain pagan-influenced thinkers of the early Christian era. The form of the dot-cluster filler motifs is typical of textiles known to have been woven during the Fatimid period which helps date this piece. The dark pink ground is also a late feature.

## 56. Rectangle Cut from a Tunic

*(Additional illustrations on page 165)*

*Colors and design:* The design motifs are contained in a roundel and a clavus. Both roundel and clavus have spiral-wave borders and contain motifs depicting human figures in violent action and spotted animals, possibly leopards. The clavus band ends in leaf-form pendants. The ornamentation is rendered in dark red-purple on a plain ground, now discolored but originally the creamy white color of undyed wool.

*Materials and construction:* Woven entirely of wool, the ground has a count of 9 x 18, the tapestry inserts, 9 x 23. Two lines of twining, double rows on paired warps, may have helped to prepare the area in which the clavus was woven and to keep it straight. The area for the roundel was prepared by weaving the ground first, leaving an open space in the warp shaped like a slice cut from one side of a circle that was of greater diameter than the planned roundel. Next the roundel was started, filling in the space on either side with yarn that matched the rest of the ground. When the shape of the roundel was established, the weaving of both ground and roundel was carried out more or less simultaneously, areas awkward for the shuttle being filled in with needle-woven tapestry. When completed, the roundel appeared enclosed in a shadowy lentoid, barely discernable, and not intended to be a decorative element. While the roundel and clavus were woven neatly enough, some details indicate carelessness on the part of the weaver; for example, one warp end was left down for nearly 10 cm before the defective heddle was noticed and corrected, and there are sections of doubled wefts that appear to be accidental, too.

*Dimensions:* 33 x 58 cm.

*Date:* Tenth century.

*Accession number:* 389-2422.

*Remarks:* Two of the figures may be enacting the story of the interrupted sacrifice of Isaac by Abraham, being observed by an angel flying overhead. The theme was a popular one in the late period, but through repetition the design became increasingly debased and nearly unrecognizable, as in the example here.

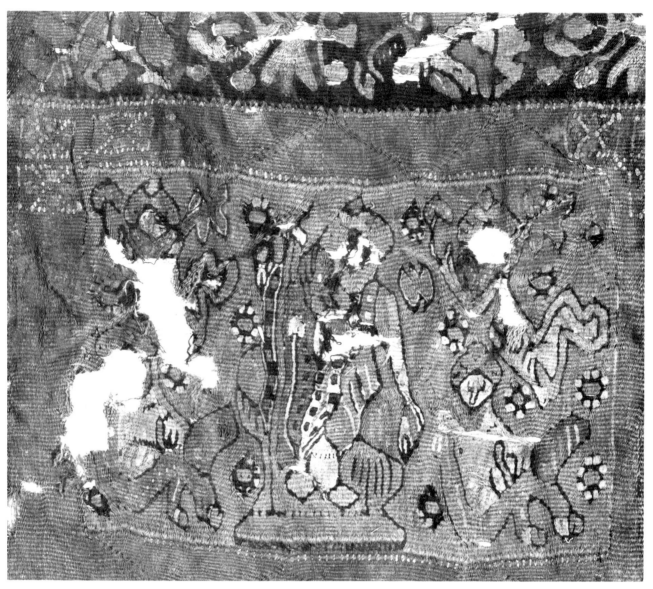

*Detail of Number 55* ↔

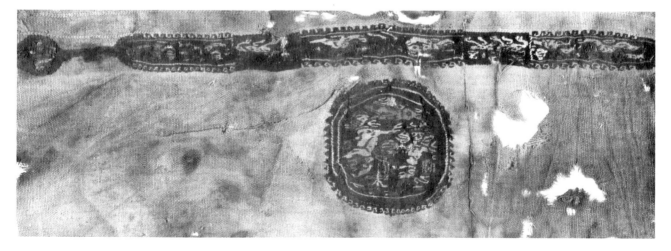

*56. Rectangle Cut from a Tunic*

## 57. Tunic Fragment with Shoulder Ornament

*Colors and design:* The ground is dark yellow. At one edge of the fragment is a segment of a plain, dark red clavus. The ornament, a roundel, has a dark brown spiral-wave border and contains the figures of two dancers, wearing only scarves, each with one upraised hand. They are worked in brown and dull orange.

*Materials and construction:* Woven entirely of wool, the ground thread count is 8 x 26, the tapestry insert, 7 x 46–50. Like the preceding example, the roundel was woven as a circle in a nearly invisible lentoid. The tips of the lentoid are tapestry, woven with the same yarn as the main ground of the tunic. On the reverse, the remains of weft floats indicate that the weft shots of the ground passed behind the tapestry portion of the textile and were completed before the ground was filled in around it.

*Dimensions:* 16.5 x 18 cm.

*Date:* Tenth century.

*Accession number:* 389-2599.

*Remarks:* For the possible symbolism of the dancers see the remarks for Number 33.

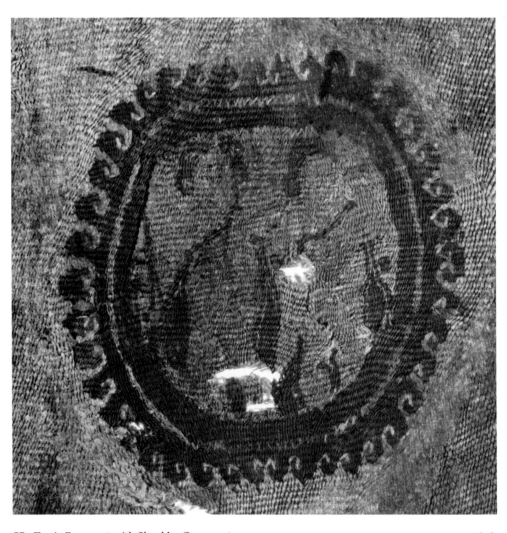

*57. Tunic Fragment with Shoulder Ornament*

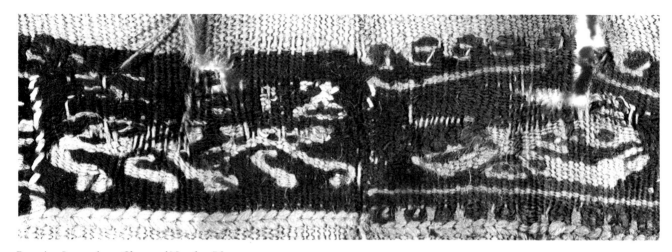

*Running Leopards on Clavus of Number 56*

*Tapestry Roundel from Shoulder Area of Number 56 with Isaac and Abraham*

## 58. Tunic Roundel from Akhmîm

*Colors and design:* The roundel has a wide, dark pink border decorated with an arcade, each arch containing a "pearl." In the center is a dark pink motif on a tan ground that may represent a man attacking a lion. There is one filler-motif, a small quatrefoil.

*Materials and construction:* Made of wool and linen weft on dyed linen warp, 7 x 50, the roundel was woven in a normal tapestry technique. The dyed warps are of three different colors, dark blue, dark yellow, and light brown, regularly arranged. Since this has no visible effect so far as the tapestry roundel is concerned, it is probable that the garment ornamented by the roundel was woven in a pattern weave, for example, a three-rod twill, which would have made effective use of the three colors.

*Dimensions:* 11.5 x 11 cm.

*Date:* Ninth century (?)

*Accession number* 389-2389.

*Remarks:* At present the roundel is mounted on a linen textile, possibly ancient, but not related to it. For information about the site, see the remarks for Number 34.

## 59. Tunic Fragment with Roundel Ornament

*Colors and design:* What remains of the tunic body is beige, while the ground of the ornament is dark yellow. The roundel carries a narrow border of rhomboids and a wider border with filler-motifs of paired dots. Within the inner circle is a formal arrangement of four birds, two chrysalises or locusts (cicadas), and two symmetrical floral motifs. In the center is a disk containing a stylized insect motif. The colors are blue-green, yellow, brown, and dull red.

*Materials and construction:* The roundel is a separate piece that was whip-stitched to the body of the tunic. The warp of the roundel lies at right angles to the warp direction of the tunic. Both parts are wool tapestry. The thread count of the body is 10 x 22, of the ornament, 6 x 48.

*Dimensions:* 14 x 18 cm.

*Date:* Ninth or tenth century.

*Accession number:* 389-2435.

*Remarks:* Insects were sometimes depicted on late antique gems. A personal or a family symbol may be represented on the Rietz textile. The unusual life cycle of some cicadas, called seventeen-year locusts, have made them symbols of longevity or immortality, an idea expressed in the myth of Tithonos. He wished for eternal life, but forgot to wish for lasting youth. Eventually he turned into a cicada and chirped on into eternity. In Plato's beautiful little dialogue about love, the *Phaedrus*, Socrates tells about cicadas, how they live without nourishment and when their time to die arrives they are able to overcome death, becoming instead messengers and informers for the Muses. Jeweled effigies of cicadas were made in the early Medieval period, perhaps in reference to one of these concepts.

58.  Tunic Roundel from Akhmîm                    ↔

59.  Tunic Fragment with Roundel Ornament

## 60. Two Fragments of a Tunic Clavus

*Colors and design:* The clavus decoration consists of rectangles with groups of dancers alternating with rectangles containing an elaborate, symmetrical flowering tree. The dancers are worked in beige, dark brown, tan, green, pink, and light blue on a medium red ground. The tree is worked in the same colors but on a tan ground. Both rectangles have dark blue borders edged with spiral waves for the dancers' panels, ornamented with linked cartouches for the tree panels.

*Materials and construction:* The weave is tapestry, wool and linen weft on linen warp, 8 x 64. The clavus appears to have been assembled by cutting a banded, tapestry-woven textile into rectangles and sewing sections from different bands together to provide ornamentation for a tunic.

*Dimensions:* 6 x 18 cm and 7 x 26 cm.

*Related example:* Baginski and Tidhar 1980:141, no. 214.

*Date:* Ninth or tenth century.

*Accession numbers:* 389-2580 and 389-2581.

*Remarks:* The dumpy little figures are barely recognizable as human forms. Their drawing contrasts greatly with that of the elaborate, symmetrical plants associated with them. At work here is the turning away from Classical canons that started around the time of the Arab conquest as a reaction against nearly everything Byzantine.

## 61. Fragment of a Tunic Clavus

*Colors and design:* The multicolor clavus band has borders of reverse scallops, each scallop containing a trefoil. The center motifs are quatrefoils and roundels in alternation. Each quatrefoil has a dot rosette, composed of nine dots, in the center. The roundels contain, respectively, a bird with a large spoon-shaped bill, the bust of a woman, robed and wearing a wreath, and a butterfly. The design motifs are worked in brown, dull medium-red, blue-green, light green, and pink on a beige ground.

*Materials and construction:* The clavus is woven in tapestry, wool and linen weft on paired linen warps, 8 x 60.

*Dimensions:* 8 x 27 cm.

*Date:* Ninth century.

*Accession number:* 389-2424.

*Remarks:* The strong degree of stylization of this piece makes its subject matter difficult to recognize at first sight. The elements of the quatrefoil are particularly obscure, but from similar, more realistic examples it can be determined that the motifs are, in fact, rolled acanthus leaves.

*60. One of Two Fragments of a Tunic Clavus*

*60. One of Two Fragments of a Tunic Clavus*

*61. Fragment of a Tunic Clavus*

## 62. Band Fragment from al-Faiyūm

*Colors and design:* One edge of this dark pink band has a dark blue zigzag border. Filler motifs are of two types, cream-colored rectangles placed on diagonals slanting in opposite directions and angular, dull yellow birds with black spots and one black bird with yellow spots. The rectangles are ornamented with motifs resembling birds with pink bodies and large yellow beaks. Spaces around the principal motifs are filled with dots and eight-petaled rosettes.

*Materials and construction:* The material is wool, woven in tapestry on two-ply Z-twist warp, 6 x 64. A surviving portion of selvedge shows that it was formed of double-paired wefts.

*Dimensions:* 45 x 9 cm.

*Related examples:* Brooklyn, Brooklyn Museum of Art acc. no. 38.754 (Thompson 1971:80, no. 35); Paris, Louvre 836 (Du Bourguet 1964:286, no. I F 105).

*Date:* Ninth or tenth century.

*Accession number:* 389-2417.

*Remarks:* al-Faiyūm is the modern name of Piom, more anciently, Arsinoë. In the Coptic period it was an important weaving center. This textile was anciently cut and sewn together so as to form either a *gamma*, a common form of tunic ornament, or a textile edging. A piece in similar style is in Brooklyn (see above). About it Thompson states, "Examples closely related in style to this textile are preserved with woven Arabic inscriptions datable to the ninth to tenth century" (Thompson 1971:80). The Rietz piece is undoubtedly of the same date.

## 63. Strip Cut from a Patterned Textile

*Colors and design:* The original textile of which this is a portion appears to have had an allover design organized around rows of battlement meander. The meander is dark blue and is decorated with six-petaled rosettes. The spaces delineated by the bends in the meander are filled with *tau* motifs, with bifurcated bases, and are flanked by large, six-petaled rosettes. The ground is tan, and the motifs are worked in black, tan, red, yellow, light blue, and pink.

*Materials and construction:* The weave is tapestry, wool and linen weft on linen two-ply Z-twist warp, 9 x 56.

*Dimensions:* 9 x 56 cm.

*Date:* Tenth century.

*Accession number:* 389-2410.

*Remarks:* Much of what characterizes Coptic art is absent from this colorful textile with its completely nonrepresentational decoration.

62. *Band Fragment from al-Faiyūm*

63. *Strip Cut from a Patterned Textile*

## 64. Fragment of a Curtain with a False Kufic Inscription

*(Color plate, page 142)*

*Colors and design:* In the center of the fragment is a polychrome insert band. It is surrounded by a dark blue area ornamented by rows of meaningless kufic letters in yellow and pink. The insert has pearl borders and contains roundels alternating with quatrefoils that may represent jeweled ornaments. The roundels contain, respectively, a bird motif, a six-pointed star, a second, different bird motif, an animal head, a building(?), a floral motif, and another star. The motifs are woven in red, medium green, yellow, light blue, pinkish white, and black.

*Materials and construction:* Woven entirely in wool, the ground is tabby, 12 x 12, the insert band, tapestry, 12 x 42. The quality of the weaving is excellent.

*Dimensions:* 17.5 x 41 cm.

*Related examples:* A wool textile with similar motifs and inscription is in New York, Metropolitan Museum of Art (Dimand 1931:89, fig. 2).

*Date:* Late tenth or early eleventh century.

*Accession number:* 389-2419.

*Remarks:* Textiles with real inscriptions were a feature of Arabic weaving from about the tenth century on. Some very fine ones were made in Egypt in the eleventh century and later. This example and a number of related pieces may represent early attempts by Coptic weavers to conform to Muslim taste.

---

## 65. Three Fragments of a Tunic

*(Illustrated on pages 174 – 175, with color plate on page 143)*

*Colors and design:* Originally the tunic had clavus bands that ran from the shoulders to the hem. At the neckline a matching band connected the clavus bands, and the usual double bands decorated the wrist area of the sleeves. All the bands are bordered by narrower bands containing lozenges and are filled with multicolored squares, each containing a fanciful, vaguely zoomorphic figure. In addition, the neck band is embellished with a row of pendant motifs. The fragments all have a discolored cream ground with decorative motifs in red, dark yellow, green, dark blue, and red-purple

*Materials and construction:* The material is wool, and the whole tunic was woven in tapestry, 7 x 28, with a few minor design details added in embroidery, worked with long stitches on the reverse side. The unused warp of the sleeve was formed into a corded edge (for a diagram illustrating the technique see Start [1914:9, fig. 6]).

*Dimensions:* Yoke fragment, 15 x 31 cm, sleeve fragment, 25 x 18.5 cm, clavus fragment, 15 x 31 cm.

*Date:* Tenth century.

*Accession numbers:* 389-2453, 389-2454, 389-2457.

*Remarks:* Possibly made for a Muslim Copt, the designs appear to avoid resemblances to living creatures and yet to give the illusion of an ordinary Coptic tunic with figured ornament. A number of native Egyptians converted to the Muslim faith, in part for the economic advantages it offered: members of the Christian faith were heavily taxed.

*Detail of Number 64*

*64. Fragment of a Curtain with a False Kufic Inscription*

65. *One of Three Fragments of a Tunic*  ↔

65. One of Three Fragments of a Tunic

65. One of Three Fragments of a Tunic

## 66. Square Tunic Ornament

*(Color plate, page 144)*

*Colors and design:* What little remains of the tunic has a dark yellow ground. The square ornament is dark blue with cream-colored motifs. It has a narrow, spiral-wave border and a center design of a small square containing a tiny Greek cross framed by a larger one in outline. Twelve squares fill the remainder of the space, each with a filler motif, hooked crosses alternating with a motif of a four-petaled rosette with symmetrical tendrils.

*Materials and construction:* The material is wool and the weave tapestry, 9 x 70. Single rows of twining accentuate some of the straight lines of the design, and the whole ornament is edged by a double row of twining.

*Dimensions:* 14 x 14 cm.

*Date:* Tenth century.

*Accession number:* 389-2434.

*Remarks:* The dark yellow ground may signify that this was made during one of the periods after the Arab Conquest when Christians were expected to wear distinctive garments. The inconspicuous cross motif and the hooked cross, a disguised form of cross, indicate that the original owner was most probably a Christian.

## 67. Section of a Tunic Sleeve

*(Illustrated on page 179, with color plate on page 145)*

*Colors and design:* The sleeve has a plain beige ground with a rectangular red-purple insert. The insert is bordered top and bottom with a band of small crosses and is divided into three parts. An oval in the middle panel contains an equal-armed cross, a lesser oval with a small cross at the center. The arms of the main cross are decorated with a stylized vine with leaves, grape clusters, and tendrils. The side panels are divided down the center by a band of small crosses and are filled with motifs that vaguely suggest crosses and anchors.

*Materials and construction:* The piece is wool, tapestry weave with different thread counts in the ground and ornament, 12 x 32 and 11 x 64. There are some embroidered details. Three selvedges are preserved. The side selvedges were woven over two warp bundles to make a firm edge. The upper selvedge was finished by twisting unused warp ends in such a way as to form a corded edge.

*Dimensions:* 24.7 x 28.4 cm.

*Date:* Eleventh century.

*Accession number:* 389-2401

*Remarks:* The somewhat obscure nature of the Christian symbols may have been a response to a ruling that required Christians to signify their religion by their dress combined with a desire on the part of the wearer to make such indicators as inconspicuous as allowable.

*66. Square Tunic Ornament*

### 68. Tunic Yoke Fragment From al-Bahnasā

*Colors and design:* The dull purple band ornament is bordered with a spiral-wave design. The interior is divided into three small bands, two plain ones framing a third containing symmetrical linear motifs representing stylized grapevines. Shortly past the point where the band turns the corner is a different motif, perhaps an amphora. These designs are worked in cream color. A small fragment of the body of the tunic remains, indicating that it was dark orange.

*Materials and construction:* The tunic was woven in the tapestry technique with wool warp and weft, 6 x 40.

*Dimensions:* 10 x 41 cm.

*Date:* Eleventh century (?)

*Accession number* 389-2411.

*Remarks:* When complete, this garment must have been both colorful and elegant with its color scheme of dull purple and dark orange. The amphora and vine symbol was a common Christian motif. Al-Bahnasā, better known as Oxyrhynchus, was one of the great weaving centers of Egypt in the Coptic period.

*68. Tunic Yoke Fragment from al-Bahnasā*

*67. Section of a Tunic Sleeve*

*Back of Number 67 showing method of securing twisted warp ends.*

## 69. Decorated Roundel from a Tunic

*Colors and design:* The dark pink ground of this piece is slightly faded (the reverse is darker than the front). The design is worked in linen that has darkened with time and dirt. The main motif is a starlike, linear floral interlace with a small, spirited lion occupying the center. Around the edge is a row of small crosses attached by their bases to the narrow band that encircles the roundel.

*Materials and construction:* The roundel is woven on two-ply Z-twist linen warp, with S-twist wool and linen weft, 11 x 76. The technique is tapestry, worked with curving wefts that follow the lines of the design.

There are long weft floats on the back. Like so many of the extant textiles, this roundel was cut from another, probably worn-out, garment and reused. The edges were turned under and the piece was attached to the new garment by rather long, judging from the spacing of the needle holes, running stitches.

*Dimensions:* 11 x 13 cm.

*Date:* Eleventh century.

*Accession number:* 389-2382.

*Remarks:* Lions, as mentioned previously, have protective attributes.

---

## 70. Oval Garment Ornament

*Colors and design:* The ornament has a wide, outer border with dark pink ground and a linear rinceau worked in linen, now beige in color, but originally white. In a smaller oval in the center is a stylized flower in a wreath of multicolored leaves, dark pink, dull yellow, and two shades of green. The ground is beige.

*Materials and construction:* The weave is tapestry with linen warp, wool and linen weft, 9 x 50. The work is exceptionally fine with short weft floats on the back.

*Dimensions:* 8.5 x 12 cm.

*Date:* Tenth century.

*Accession number:* 389-2384.

*Remarks:* Multicolored leaves arranged in bands or garlands form a common motif in architectural mosaics. An early example appears in the mausoleum of Galla Placidia at Ravenna, Italy, built in the fifth century. The textile version is more rigid and is certainly later in date.

*69. Decorated Roundel from a Tunic*

*70. Oval Garment Ornament*

## 71. Mantle or Coverlet Fragment

*Colors and design:* The design is organized into bands, decorated ones interspersed with plain ones. Two bands contain quatrefoils with leaf motifs filling the triangular spaces between the quatrefoils. The third band is half as wide as the other two and is decorated with triangles and leaves. It is in fact a repeat of half the design of the other two bands divided down the center.

*Materials and construction:* Tapestry, woven entirely in wool, 9 x 22. One edge is corded.

*Dimensions:* 22 x 89 cm.

*Date:* Eleventh or twelfth century.

*Accession number:* 389-2582.

*Remarks:* This piece may be Islamic in origin, though not too different, technically, from Coptic work.

---

## 72. Fragment of a Decorated Textile

*Colors and design:* This multicolored square ornament is composed of geometric motifs. In the center is a circle framed by a square. In each corner a smaller circle is connected to the middle square by a short length of cable pattern. A band containing a braid connects the small roundels at top and bottom, a wider band with a species of twined pattern connects the roundels at the sides. The middle circle is filled with small geometric motifs, the outer circles by lozenges.

*Materials and construction:* The piece is tapestry weave with linen warp and wool and linen weft, 8 x 32.

*Dimensions:* 16 x 12.5 cm.

*Date:* Eleventh or twelfth century.

*Accession number:* 389-2393.

*Remarks:* The design bears a resemblance to designs found on some early medieval jeweled book covers.

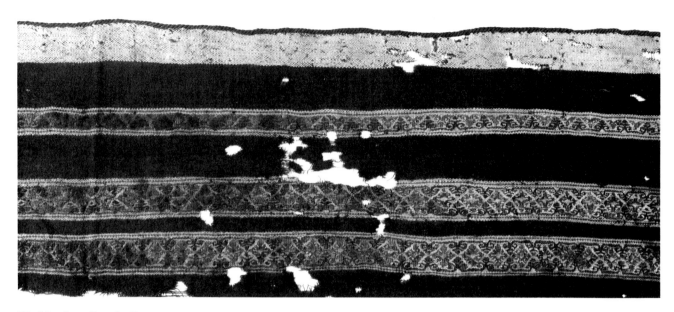

71. *Mantle or Coverlet Fragment*

72. *Fragment of a Decorated Textile*

# VII. GLOSSARY

**Adjective dyestuff**. Commonly, a water-soluble dye that must be applied in connection with a **mordant** in order to develop and permanently fix the color to the fibers boiled or steeped in a solution of the dyestuff. Less commonly, a dyestuff that is insoluble in water. See **vat dye**.

**Aedicula**, pl. **aediculae**. A small structure used as a shrine; sometimes represented in Coptic textiles to signify that the enclosed figures have spiritual significance.

**Arabesque**. An intricate decorative motif; regular or irregular in shape; usually repeated at least twice in the same form.

**Artificial shed**. The second of the two sheds used in **plain weave**. It is formed by the **heddle**.

**Band**. A color division in the **weft** direction.

**Beater**. A device used to drive the **weft** into place after the **shot** has been made. There are several types. The simplest is the so-called weaver's sword, a heavy, wedge-shaped batten. See also **reed**.

**Boat shuttle**. A **shuttle** with a hollow elliptical shape, the form of which suggests a boat with identical ends. Inside is a removable rod around which the **weft** is wound.

**Breast beam**. The beam nearest the weaver on a horizontal **loom**. It performs the same function as the **cloth beam**.

**Cable**. See **Guilloche**.

**Cartouche**. A figure enclosing a space either symmetrical or eccentric in outline. The cartouche may be blank or it may contain a motif.

**Clavus**, pl. **clavi**. In Coptic garment ornament, clavi are the vertical tapestry bands descending from the shoulder areas of a tunic. They are of varying lengths, in some examples they extend from the shoulders to the hem of the garment, in others they end around the waist level, terminating in a simple decorative motif, a roundel or a leaf shape.

**Cloth beam**. The beam on which the finished cloth is rolled. It is the principal beam of the upright warp-weighted loom and is approximately level with the standing weaver's head, or a little higher. On two-beamed upright looms it is the one nearer the floor.

**Counter-shed**. See **artificial shed**.

**Crapaud**. A decorative technique carried out in **weft** floats. The lines of the ornament leap freely from place to place, often crossing above several wefts at a time. It is sometimes mistaken for embroidery. The technique is also called **ressort**, and, more commonly, **flying needle** or **flying shuttle**.

**Dalmatic**. A long-sleeved garment of Eastern origin, by tradition introduced to the West by Emperor Elagabalus (218–222). At first rejected by the Romans as effete, it eventually became the common garment of the Roman world, including the Coptic part of it. See **tunic**.

**Drawloom**. In the Coptic region, a **loom** for weaving textiles with rows of identical yet rather simple-appearing angular figures of men, plants, animals, and geometric designs, all composed of block-shaped units. The pattern rows can be repeated as often as desired. This is accomplished by preparing the loom so that the **warps** required for the pattern blocks can be lifted in groups, a specially tailored group for each **shot**. The warp groups vary from shot to shot in order to build the the design. The groups are lifted in a set order as the weaving proceeds. Once the warp is prepared the designs are produced automatically as long as the correct groups are selected by the person assisting the weaver, the draw boy. The weaver cannot alter or vary the design except by changing the threading of the loom.

**Flying needle.** See **crapaud**.

**Flying shuttle.** A decorative technique. Not to be confused with the mechanically propelled shuttle, invented in 1733 by John Kay, called the flying shuttle. **See crapaud.**

**Foot-powered loom.** A **loom** with one or more **heddles** attached to cords with stirrups or treadles so the **sheds** can be changed with the feet. Technically, this is a **hand loom** though it is worked with the feet as well as the hands. See **hand loom**.

**Gammulae.** L-shaped, angular ornaments resembling the Greek capital letter gamma (Γ). They generally occur in pairs on Coptic textiles.

**Genius**, pl. **genii**. Supernatural beings in human form, often shown with wings though able to fly perfectly well without them.

**Guilloche.** A continuous pattern composed of two or more interlacing curved lines. Also called a **cable**.

**Hand loom.** Any **loom** powered by human muscles rather than water, steam, or electricity. See also **foot-powered loom**.

**Harness.** The rectangular frame and its rigging that carries the **heddles** on developed forms of **hand looms**.

**Heddle.** A device of string, wire, or wood used to control a single **warp** thread. Sets of them are used to form the **sheds** in weaving. Only one set, attached to alternate **warp** threads, is needed for **plain weave**, but two or more sets are needed for **pattern weaves**. The word can also refer to any device used to hold or support sets of individual heddles, such as the **heddle-rod**.

**Heddle-rod.** A smooth stick, a little longer than the width of the loom, to which the **heddles** are attached. It was used on **hand looms** in many places and periods before the invention and distribution of the **harness**. Activating it forms the **artificial shed**.

**Heddle-stick.** See **heddle-rod**.

**High-warp loom.** Any **loom** with the **warp** set on a more or less vertical plane. The expression is derived from the French tapestry weavers' term, *haute-lisse*, for this variety of loom.

**Laze-rod.** A smooth stick woven into the **warp** to help keep it taut and in order. Generally used in pairs.

**Loom.** A structure made to hold a **warp** in position for weaving that is also equipped with at least one **heddle**.

**Low-warp loom.** Any **loom** with the **warp** set on a horizontal plane. Also termed *basse-lisse,* from the terminology of French tapestry weavers.

**Mordant.** Usually a water-soluble metallic salt applied to a fiber in connection with a dyestuff for the purpose of developing the color of the dye and permanently fixing it to the fiber.

**Natural shed.** The first of the two basic **sheds** formed on **hand looms**. On many looms it is created when the loom is warped and is formed automatically, or naturally, when the **heddle** is released.

**Orans**, pl. **orantes**. A standing human figure with both hands upraised often depicted in Early Christian art. The attitude is one of adoration or supplication. A variant form in which only one hand is raised appears frequently in Coptic textile design.

**Orbiculae.** The round or oval ornaments inset on the shoulders and at the level of the hips or knees of a garment.

**Pallium**, pl. **palli**. The Coptic male outer garment. It was either worn loose or fastened on the right shoulder with a fibula.

**Paragauda.** The hem border of a tunic.

**Pattern weave.** A weave in which the **wefts** and **warps** skip over two or more threads at regular intervals, forming a pattern that repeats evenly over the entire surface of the textile. Twills are the most common type of pattern weave, but there are many others including the elaborate repeat designs produced by **drawlooms**.

**Patterned textile.** A textile in either **plain weave** or **pattern weave** ornamented with designs worked in one or more colors.

**Plain weave.** The basic weave. Every thread, **warp** or **weft**, passes under every second thread in its path. **Rep** and **tapestry** were the principal plain weaves used by Coptic weavers.

**Reed.** A rectangular frame holding many closely spaced strips of cane, wood, or metal. All of the **warp** ends pass through the spaces between the strips. It performs two functions: it keeps the warp evenly spaced during weaving and, by drawing it firmly against the edge of the completed weaving after each **shot**, it beats the **weft** into place.

**Rep**. A type of **plain weave** in which there are more **warps** than **wefts** to the centimeter of completed cloth and in which the warp bends more than the weft. Also called ribbed **tabby**.

**Ressort**. See **crapaud**.

**Rinceau**. A continuous pattern in the form of a vine. It is an inhabited rinceau if curling stalks or tendrils enclose figures of humans or animals.

**Rod-heddle**. See **heddle-rod**.

**Rolag**. A cylindrical mass of wool, uniform in density and disposition of fibers, specially prepared for spinning **woolen yarn**.

**Rove**. A loosely compacted roll of fibers prepared for spinning **worsted yarn**.

**Shadow band**. A decoration composed of several **weft** bundles of the same yarn used for the rest of the cloth. It appears as a **band** of ridges.

**Shed**. The space made when the **warp** threads are divided for the **shot**.

**Shed-rod**. The stick that controls the **natural shed** on a simple **loom**. It is commonly a flat slat, a little longer than the width of the **warp**, and is manipulated by turning it on edge. It may double as the **beater**.

**Shed-stick**. See **shed-rod**.

**Shot**. A single passage of the **weft** through a **shed**.

**Shuttle**. A device for storing a length of **weft** in a compact way so it may be passed through the **shed**.

**Soumak weave**. A decorative technique in which the **weft** thread wraps around the **warps**.

**Stripe**. A color division in the **warp** direction.

**Substantive dyestuff**. A dyestuff that is complete in itself. Its color will become permanently fixed on fibers boiled or steeped in a solution of the dyestuff alone without the addition of a mordant.

**Tabby**. A type of **plain weave** in which there are relatively the same number of **warps** and **wefts** to the centimeter of completed cloth and in which both warp and weft bend. Rare in Egyptian weaving.

**Tapestry**. A type of **plain weave** with less **warp** than **weft** to the centimeter. The weft often turns back within the row and is not thrown from selvedge to selvedge.

**Thread count**. The number of **warps** and **wefts** in a square centimeter of finished cloth, for example, 8 x 32. The warp count is stated first.

**Tunic**. In the literature relating to Coptic textiles, a simple straight-sided gown with sleeves; in fact, the **dalmatic**, but rarely called so.

**Vat dye**. An insoluble **adjective dyestuff** that requires special treatment before it can be used. The details of the process vary with the dyestuff, but the goal of the process is to first render the dyestuff soluble so it can be applied to the fibers, than to change it back to its insoluble form so the color will be permanent and not lost when the textile is laundered.

**Warp**. The **yarn** running lengthwise through a woven fabric. The term also connotes the sheet of **yarns** laid together on a beam. Warp direction other than vertical is indicated by the symbol ↔ under textile illustrations.

**Warp beam**. The beam that holds the unused **warp**. Not present on warp-weighted looms.

**Web**. A textile as it is being woven on a **loom**.

**Weft**. The **yarn** extending from selvedge to selvedge at right angles to the **warp**.

**Woolen yarn**. Yarn made from carded wool fibers, generally short staple, in which the fibers are predominantly at right angles to the length of the yarn.

**Worsted yarn**. Yarn made from long-staple wool fibers prepared for spinning by combing, which arranges the fibers parallel to the length of the yarn.

**Yarn**. A generic term for an assemblage of fibers twisted or laid together to form a continuous strand suitable for use in weaving.

For words not listed here, or for additional information, see Forbes (1956:183–188) and Emery (1966).

# BIBLIOGRAPHY

Alexander, S. M. 1978. Information on Historical Techniques, Textiles: I. Classical Authors. Art and Archaeology Technical Abstracts 15 (2):344–380.

Allen, T.W. [1919] 1951. Homeri opera. Vol. 4. Odysseae, books 13–24. Clarendon Press, Oxford. Not paginated.

Atiya, A. S. 1968. A History of Eastern Christianity. Methuen, London. 486 pp.

Badawy, A. 1978. Coptic art and archaeology: The art of the Christian Egyptians from the Late Antique to the Middle Ages. Harvard University Press, Cambridge, Massachusetts. 387 pp.

Baginski, A. and A. Tidhar. 1980. Textiles from Egypt, 4th–13th centuries C.E. L. A. Mayer Memorial Institute for Islamic Art, Jerusalem. 176 pp.

Bagnall, R. S. and A. E. Samuel. 1976. Ostraka in the Royal Ontario Museum 2. American Studies in Papyrology 15. Hakkert, Toronto. xii + 147 pp.

Bailey, K. C. 1925. The dyeing of the ancient Romans according to the description in Pliny's Historia Naturalis. Chem. Ind. 44:1135.

Barber, E. J. W. 1982. New Kingdom Egyptian textiles: Embroidery vs. Weaving. Am. J. Archaeol. 86:442–445.

Barns, J. W. B. 1966. The Oxyrhynchus Papyri 31. The British Academy Egyptian Exploration Fund, London. 151 pp.

Barraclough, G., ed. 1979. The Times atlas of world history. Times Books, London. 360 pp.

Beazley, J. D. 1956. Attic black-figure vase-painters. Clarendon Press, Oxford. 851 pp.

Bell, H. I. 1948. Egypt from Alexander the Great to the Arab Conquest: A study in the diffusion and decay of Hellenism. Clarendon Press, Oxford. 168 pp.

_____. 1975. Cults and creeds in Graeco-Roman Egypt. Ares, Chicago. 117 pp.

Bellinger, L. 1956. Textile analysis: Pile techniques in Egypt and the Near East. Textile Museum: Workshop Notes No. 12. Textile Museum, Washington D.C. 8 pp.

_____. 1959. Craft habits, Part 1: Loom types suggested by weaving details. Textile Museum: Workshop Notes No. 19. Textile Museum, Washington D.C. 6 pp.

Bendinelli, G. 1921. An underground tomb with important fresco decoration recently discovered in Rome. Art and Archaeol. 11:169–172.

Betz, H.D. ed. 1986. The Greek magical papyri in translation. Univ. of Chicago Press, Chicago and London. 339 pp.

Blegen, C. W., J. L. Caskey, and M. Rawson. 1950. Troy: General introduction, the first and second settlements. Princeton Univ. Press, Princeton. 396 pp.

Blum, R. and E. Blum. 1970. The dangerous hour: The lore of crisis and mystery in rural Greece. Charles Scribner's Sons, New York. 410 pp.

Brooklyn Museum. 1941. Pagan and Christian Egypt: Egyptian art from the first to the tenth century A.D. Brooklyn Museum, New York. 86 pp.

Broudy, E. 1979. The book of looms. Studio Vista (Cassell), London. 187 pp.

Browning, R. 1976. The Emperor Julian. Univ. of California Press, Berkeley and Los Angeles. 256 pp.

Brunton, G. and G. Caton-Thompson. 1928. The Badarian civilisation and predynastic remains near Badari. Egyptian Research Account Publications, London. 128 pp.

Burnham, D. K. 1972. Coptic knitting: An ancient technique. Textile History 3:116–124.

Bury, J. B. [1908] 1958. The ancient Greek historians. Reprint. Dover, New York. 281 pp.

Carroll, D. L. 1965. Patterned textiles in Greek art. Ph.D. Dissertation, Univ. of California, Los Angeles. University Microfilms, Ann Arbor, Michigan. 443 pp.

_____. 1973. An Etruscan Textile in Newark. Am. J. Archaeol. 77:334–336.

_____. 1983. Warping the Greek loom: A second method. Am. J. Archaeol. 87:96–98.

_____. 1985. Dating the foot-powered loom: The Coptic evidence. Am. J. Archaeol. 89:168–173.

Caton-Thompson, G. and E. W. Gardner. 1934. The desert Fayum. Royal Anthropological Institute of Great Britain and Ireland, London. I text, II plates.

Cipolla, C. M. and D. Birdsall. 1979. The technology of man: A visual history. Holt, Rinehart and Winston, New York. 271 pp.

Cirlot, J. E. 1962. A dictionary of symbols. J. Sage, translator. Philosophical Library, New York. 400 pp.

Clédat, J. 1904. Le monastère et nécropole de Baouît. Mémoires de l'Insititut français d'archéologie orientale du Caire No. 12. Cairo. vii + 164 pp.

Coles, R. A. 1970. The Oxyrhynchus papyri 36. The British Academy Egyptian Exploration Fund, London. 115 pp.

Crawford, M. and J. Reynolds. 1977. The Aezani copy of the prices edict. Zeitschrift für Papyrologie und Epigraphik 26:125–151.

Crowfoot, G. M. 1931. Methods of hand spinning in Egypt and the Sudan. Bankfield Museum Notes No. 12. F. King and Sons, Halifax. 51 pp.

Davies, N. de. 1902. The rock tombs of Deir el Gabrawi, Vol. II. Egyptian Exploration Fund, London. vii + 43.

Dimand, M. S. 1931. Coptic and Egypto-Arabic textiles. Bulletin of the Metropolitan Museum of Art 26:89–91.

Dodds, E. R. 1965. Pagan and Christian in an age of anxiety. University Press, Cambridge, England. 144 pp.

Dorigo, W. 1971. Late Roman painting. Praeger, New York. 345 pp.

Du Bourguet, P. 1964. Musée national du Louvre. Catalogue des etoffes Coptes, Vol. 1. Editions des musées nationaux, Paris. 672 pp.

_____. 1971. Art of the Copts. C. Hay-Shaw, translator. Crown, New York. 234 pp.

Edgar, C. C. 1925. Zenon Papyri I: Catalogue général des antiquités égyptiennes du Musée du Caire, vol. 79, nos. 59001–59139. L'institut Français d'archéologie orientale, Cairo. vii + 180 pp.

_____. 1926. Zenon Papyri II: Catalogue général des antiquités égyptiennes du Musée du Caire, vol. 79, nos. 59140–59297. L'institut Français d'archéologie orientale, Cairo. viii + 201 pp.

_____. 1928. Zenon Papyri III: Catalogue général des antiquités égyptiennes du Musée du Caire, vol. 85, nos. 59298–59531. L'institut Français d'archéologie orientale, Cairo. 291 pp.

Elworthy, F. T. [1895] 1970. The evil eye: The origins and practices of superstition. Reprint. Collier-Macmillan, London. 471 pp.

Emery, I. 1966. The primary structures of fabrics: An illustrated classification. The Textile Museum, Washington D.C. 339 pp.

Forbes, R. J. 1956. Studies in ancient technology. Vol. 4. E. J. Brill, Leiden. 257 pp.

Frank, T. 1940. An economic survey of ancient Rome V: Rome and Italy of the empire. The Johns Hopkins Press, Baltimore. 445 pp.

Friedländer, P. 1945. Documents of dying paganism: Textiles of late antiquity in Washington, New York, and Leningrad. Univ. of California Press, Berkeley and Los Angeles. 66 pp.

Gervers, V. 1977. An early Christian curtain in the Royal Ontario Museum. Pp. 68–70 in Studies in textile history in memory of H. B. Burnham. V. Gervers, ed. Royal Ontario Museum, Toronto.

Godley, A. D. 1975. Herodotus with an English translation, Vol. 1. Harvard Univ. Press, Cambridge, Massachusetts. 503 pp.

Golombek, L. and V. Gervers. 1977. Tiraz fabrics in the Royal Ontario Museum. Pp. 82–125 in Studies in textile history in memory of H. B. Burnham. V. Gervers, ed. Royal Ontario Museum, Toronto.

Gow, A. S. F. 1950. Theocritus I: Introduction, text, and translation. Cambridge University, Cambridge. 257 pp.

Grabar, A. 1966. Byzantium from the death of Theodosius to the rise of Islam. S. Gilbert and J. Emmons, translators. Thames and Hudson, London. 416 pp.

Graser, E. R. 1940. The edict of Diocletian on maximum prices. Pp. 307–421 in An economic survey of ancient Rome, Vol. 5. T. Frank. The Johns Hopkins Press, Baltimore.

Grenfell, B. P. and A. S. Hunt. 1898. The Oxyrhynchus Papyri, Vol. 1. The British Academy Egyptian Exploration Fund, London. 349 pp.

_____. 1899. The Oxyrhynchus Papyri, Vol. 2. The British Academy Egyptian Exploration Fund, London. 358 pp.

Grenfell, B. P., A. S. Hunt, and D. G. Hogarth. 1900. Fayum towns and their Papyri. The British Academy Egyptian Exploration Fund, London. xvi + 374 pp.

Grenfell, B. P., A. S. Hunt, J. G. Smyly, E. J. Goodspeed, and C. C. Edgar. 1907. The Tebtunis papyri, Vol. 2. Henry Frowde, London. 484 pp.

Griffith, F. L. and H. Thompson. [1904] 1974. The Leyden papyrus: An Egyptian magical book. Reprint. Dover, New York. 205 pp.

Grube, E. J. 1962. Studies in the survival and continuity of pre-Muslim traditions in Egyptian Islamic art. J. Am. Res. Center in Egypt 1:75–84.

Gulick, C. B. [1927] 1969. Athenaeus: The Deipnosophists, Vol. 1. Reprint. Harvard Univ. Press, Cambridge, Massachusetts. 204 pp.

_____. [1928] 1967. Athenaeus: The Deipnosophists, Vol. 2. Reprint. Harvard Univ. Press, Cambridge, Massachusetts. 533 pp.

_____. [1933] 1980. Athenaeus: The Deipnosophists, Vol. 5. Reprint. Harvard Univ. Press, Cambridge, Massachusetts. 550 pp.

Gummere, R. M. 1918. Seneca: Ad Lucilium Epistulae Morales, Vol. 2. William Heinemann, New York. 479 pp.

Hoffmann, M. 1964. The warp weighted loom: Studies in the history and technology of an ancient implement. Studia Norvegica, No. 14. Oslo.

_____. 1977. Manndalen revisited: Traditional weaving in an old Lappish community in transition. Pp. 149–159 in Studies in textile history in memory of H. B. Burnham, V. Gervers, ed. Royal Ontario Museum, Toronto.

Hollen, N. and J. Saddler. 1964. Textiles. 2nd Ed. The Macmillan Company, New York. 225 pp.

Hunt A. S. and C. C. Edgar. 1932. Select papyri with an English translation. Vol. 1, Non-literary papyri: Private affairs. Harvard Univ. Press, Cambridge, Massachusetts. 452 pp.

_____. 1934. Select papyri with an English translation. Vol. 2, Non-literary papyri: Public documents. Harvard Univ. Press, Cambridge, Massachusetts. 607 pp.

Hunt, A. S. and J. G. Smyly. 1933. The Tebtunis papyri, Vol. 3. Humphrey Milford, London. 333 pp.

Johnson, A. C. 1936. An economic survey of ancient Rome. Vol. 2, Roman Egypt to the reign of Diocletian. The Johns Hopkins Press, Baltimore. 732 pp.

Jones, A. H. M. 1963. The social background of the struggle between Paganism and Christianity. Pp. 17–37 in The conflict between paganisn and Christianity in the fourth century, A. Momigliano, ed. Clarendon Press, Oxford. 218 pp.

_____. 1964. The later Roman Empire 284–602, Vol. 1. Basil Blackwell, Oxford. 522 pp.

Jones, W. H. S. [1963] 1975. Pliny: Natural History, Vol. 7, books 27–32. Reprint. Harvard Univ. Press. Cambridge, Massachusetts. 596 pp.

Kendrick, A. F. 1920. Victoria and Albert Museum, Department of Textiles. Catalogue of textiles from burying-grounds in Egypt. Vol. 1, Graeco-Roman Period. Victoria and Albert Museum, London. 142 pp.

_____. 1921. Victoria and Albert Museum, Department of Textiles. Catalogue of textiles from burying-grounds in Egypt Vol. 2, Period of transition and of Christian emblems. London. 108 pp.

_____. 1922. Victoria and Albert Museum, Department of Textiles. Catalogue of textiles from burying-grounds in Egypt. Vol. 3, Coptic period. Victoria and Albert Museum, London. 107 pp.

Ker, W. C. A. 1919. Martial: Epigrams II. William Heinemann, London. 567 pp.

Kybalova, L. 1967. Coptic textiles. Paul Hamlyn, London. 157 pp.

Lagercrantz, O. 1913. Papyrus Graecus Holmiensis: Recepte für Silber, Steine und Purpur. Vilhem Ekmans universitets fond, Uppsala. 247 pp.

Lauffer, S. 1971. Diokletians Preisedikt. Walter de Gruyter and Co., Berlin. 361 pp.

Lenzen, V. 1960. The triumph of Dionysos on textiles of late antique Egypt. Univ. of Calif. Publ. in Classical Archaeol. 5:1–38.

Levi, D. 1947. Antioch mosaic pavements Vol. 1. Publications of the Committee for the Excavation of Antioch and its Vicinity, Princeton, New Jersey. 240 pp.

Lewis, S. 1969. Early Coptic textiles: Stanford Art Gallery. Department of Art of Stanford University, Stanford, California. 87 pp.

Lindsay, W. M. 1913. Sexti Pompei Festi: De verborum significatu quae supersunt cum Pauli epitome. Teubner, Leipzig. 573 pp.

Lubell, C., ed. 1976a. Textile collections of the world. Vol. 1, United States and Canada. Van Nostrand Reinhold Co., New York. 336 pp.

_____. 1976b. Textile collections of the world. Vol. 2, United Kingdom and Ireland. Van Nostrand Reinhold Co., New York. 240 pp.

_____. 1977. Textile collections of the world. Vol. 3, France. Van Nostrand Reinhold Co., New York. 240 pp.

Lucas, A. 1962. Ancient Egyptian materials and industries. 4th ed. Rev. and enl., J. R. Harris. Edward Arnold, London. 523 pp.

McCarren, V. P. 1980. Michigan Papyri 14: American Studies in Papyrology 22, The Scholar's Press, Chico. 68 pp.

Mace, A. C. 1922. Loom weights in Egypt. Ancient Egypt 1922–23:75–76.

Meyer, P. M. 1911. Griechische Papyrusurkunden der Hamburger Staats-und Universitätsbibliothek, Vol. 1. B. G. Teubner, Leipzig-Berlin. 100 pp.

Monro. D. B. and T. W. Allen. [1920] 1954. Homeri opera. Vol. 1, Iliadis, books 1–12. Clarendon Press, Oxford. Not paginated.

Morey, C. 1942. Early Christian art. Princeton Univ. Press, Princeton. 282 pp.

Nelson, C. A. 1979. Status declarations in Roman Egypt. American Studies in Papyrology 19. Hakkert, Amsterdam. 88 pp.

Newberry, P. E. 1894. El Bersheh, Vol. 1. Egyptian Exploration Fund, London. 43 pp., 70 pl.

Newman, S. B. and H. F. Riddell. 1954. The drying twist in plant fibers. Textile Res. J. 24(2)113–117.

Norris. H. 1944. Church vestments: Their origin and development. J. M. Dent and Sons, London. 190 pp.

Pagels, E. 1981. The Gnostic gospels. Random House, New York. 214 pp.

Paolucci, A. 1978. Ravenna. Scala, Florence. 96 pp.

Perrin, B. 1920. Plutarch's "Lives," Vol. 9. William Heinemann, London. 619 pp.

Petrie, W. M. F. 1909. The arts and crafts of ancient Egypt. Edinburgh and London. xv + 157 pp.

_____. 1889. Hawara, Biahmu and Arsinoë. Field and Tuer, London. 66 pp.

_____. [1917] 1974. Tools and weapons illustrated by the Egyptian collection in University College. Aris and Phillips, Warminster, Wiltshire, England. 71 pp.

Pfister, R. 1934. Textiles de Palmyre, Vol. 1. Editions d'Art et d'Histoire, Paris. 76 pp.

_____. 1935. Teinture et alchimie dans l'orient hellenistique. Recueil d'études, archeologie, histoire d'art, études byzantines 7:1–59.

_____. 1937. Textiles de Palmyre, Vol. 2. Editions d'Art et d'Histoire, Paris. 56 pp.

_____. 1940. Textiles de Palmyre, Vol. 3. Editions d'Art et d'Histoire, Paris. 102 pp.

_____. 1948. Le role de l'Iran dans les textiles d'Antinoe. Ars Islamica 13–14:46–74.

_____. 1951. Textiles de Halabiyeh (Zenobia). P. Geuthner, Paris. 74 pp.

Pfister, R. and L. Bellinger. 1945. Textiles. Pp. 1–4, The Excavations at Dura Europos, Final Report, Vol. 4, Part 2, M. I. Rostofsteff. Yale Univ. Press, New Haven, Connecticut.

Preaux, C. 1935. Les Ostraca grecs de la collection Charles-Edwin Wilbour au Musée de Brooklyn. The Brooklyn Museum, New York. 125 pp.

Rackham, H. [1950] 1961. Pliny: Natural History Vol. 5, books 17–19. Reprint. Harvard Univ. Press, Cambridge, Massachusetts. 544 pp.

_____. [1940] 1967. Pliny: Natural History Vol. 3, books 8-11. Reprint. Harvard Univ. Press, Cambridge, Massachusetts. 544 pp.

_____. [1952] 1968. Pliny: Natural History Vol. 9, books 33-35. Reprint. Harvard Univ. Press, Cambridge, Massachusetts. 421 pp.

Riboud, K. 1977. A closer view of early Chinese silks. Pp. 252–270 *in* Studies in Textile History in Memory of H. B. Burnham, V. Gervers, ed. Royal Ontario Museum, Toronto.

Riefstahl, E. 1941. Egyptian textiles of the Graeco-Roman and early Christian period. Pp. 45–86 *in* Pagan and Christian Egypt. The Brooklyn Museum, New York.

_____. 1944. Patterned Textiles in Pharaonic Egypt: The Brooklyn Museum of Arts and Sciences. The Brooklyn Museum, New York. 56 pp.

Robinson, D. 1945. A new Attic onos or epinetron. Am. J. of Archaeol. 49:480.

Robinson, J. M, ed. [1977] 1981. The Nag Hammadi Library in English. Paperback reprint. Harper and Row, San Francisco. 491 pp.

Romer, J. 1984. Ancient lives: Daily life in Egypt of the pharaohs. Holt Rinehart and Winston, New York. 235 pp.

Roth, H. L. [1918] 1950. Studies in primitive looms. Revised reprint. Bankfield Museum, Halifax. 150 pp.

_____. [1913] 1951. Ancient Egyptian and Greek looms. Corrected reprint. Bankfield Museum, Halifax. 44 pp.

Rouse, W. H. D. 1940. Nonnos, Vol. 2. Harvard Univ. Press, Cambridge, Massachusetts. 547 pp.

Samuel, A. E. 1971. Death and taxes: Ostraka in the Royal Ontario Museum, Vol. 1. American Studies in Papyrology No. 10. Hakkert, Toronto. xiv + 151 pp.

Shurinova, R. 1967. Coptic textiles: Collection of Coptic textiles, State Pushkin Museum of Fine Arts. (In Russian with English summary of text and a bilingual catalogue.) Avrova, Leningrad. xxiii + 181 pp.

Start, L. E. 1914. Coptic cloths. Bankfield Museum Notes no. 4. F. King and Sons, Halifax. 35 pp.

Stephani, L. 1881. Erklärung einiger Kunstwerke der kaiserlichen Ermitage und anderer Sammlungen. Compte-rendu de la Commission Impériale Archéologique pour les années 1878 et 1879, Supplement. xviii + 182 pp.

Thompson, D. 1971. Coptic textiles in the Brooklyn Museum. The Brooklyn Museum, Brooklyn, New York. 101 pp.

Trendall, A. D. 1967. Red-figured vases of Lucania, Campania and Sicily. Vol. 1, Text. Clarendon Press, Oxford. 699 pp.

Trever, C. 1932. Excavations in northern Mongolia. Mem. of the Acad. Hist. Material Culture 3:1–73.

Trilling, J. 1982. The Roman heritage: Textiles from Egypt and the eastern Mediterranean 300 to 600 A.D. Textile Mus. J. 21:1–112.

Turner, E. G. 1968. Greek papyri: An introduction. Princeton Univ. Press, Princeton, New Jersey. 220 pp.

Usher, A. P. 1954. A history of mechanical inventions. Harvard Univ. Press, Cambridge, Massachusetts. 450 pp.

Vogt, E. 1937. Geflechte und Gewebe der Steinzeit. Bürkhäuser, Basel. iv + 122 pp.

Walbank, F. W. 1952. Trade and industry under the later Roman Empire in the west. Pp. 33–85 *in* Cambridge economic history of Europe. Vol. 2, Trade and industry in the Middle Ages. The University Press, Cambridge.

Walters, B. 1982. The restoration of an Orphic temple in England. Archaeology 35:36–43.

Ward, A., J. Cherry, C. Gere, and B. Cartlidge. 1981. Rings through the ages. Rizzoli, New York. 214 pp.

Wessel, K. 1965. Coptic art. McGraw-Hill Book Co., New York. 247 pp.

Wheeler, M. 1955. Rome beyond the imperial frontiers. Pelican Books, London. 224 pp.

White, R. J. 1975. The interpretation of dreams: Oneirocritica by Artemidorus. Noyes Press, Park Ridge, New Jersey. 259 pp.

Wilcken, U. 1899. Griechische Ostraka aus Aegypten und Nubien, Vol. 2. Giesecke und Devrient, Leipzig-Berlin. 497 pp.

Wild, J.-P. 1984. Some early silk finds in northwest Europe. Textile Museum J. 23:17–23.

Wilson, L. M. 1938. The clothing of the ancient Romans. The Johns Hopkins University Studies in Archaeology 24. Johns Hopkins Press, Baltimore. xiii + 178 pp.

Winlock, H. E. 1922. Heddle-jacks of Middle Kingdom looms. Ancient Egypt 1922:71–74.

_____. 1926. The monastery of Epiphanius at Thebes. Vol. 1, The archaeological material. Metropolitan Museum of Art, New York. xxvi + 276 pp.

# ACKNOWLEDGMENTS

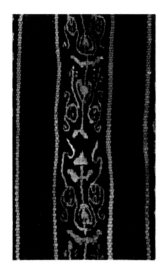

IN THE SEVEN YEARS since I wrote my first grant proposal for this volume, I have been assisted by many members of the staff of the California Academy of Sciences, by professionals in my field, by generous volunteers, and by reviewers from outside the Academy.

The original project director, Dr. Dorothy K. Washburn, first encouraged me in the planning of this project. Barbara Barton offered assistance in the preparation of the grant proposal as Curatorial Assistant and Department Secretary. Dr. Robert Sayers became interim Chairman (and later Collections Manager), and assisted me a great deal as the second project director. Dr. Linda S. Cordell, who is currently Anthropology Department Chairman, has continued to encourage me, to offer department office space, and use of equipment and services.

The library staff of CAS, especially Lesley Segedy and James Jackson, provided kind assistance in locating hard-to-find materials.

The publication staff of CAS, including Dr. Daphne G. Fautin, Scientific Publications Editor, Janet Cox, Editor of *Pacific Discovery* magazine, Katherine Ulrich, and Mary Christine Cunningham, assisted me a great deal throughout the entire publication process. Ruth Weine kindly volunteered to copy edit the manuscript and compile the index.

Susan Middleton and staff in the Photography Department worked closely and patiently with me to prepare the fine photographs for this catalog.

Dr. Elizabeth Barber and Dr. James Trilling read the manuscript and made numerous corrections and suggestions, many of which were incorporated into the manuscript.

A special thank you to Dr. Marta Hoffmann for informing me of an interesting textile in Copenhagen.

I have been encouraged throughout my career by Dr. Darrell A. Amyx, now Professor Emeritus of the History of Art at the University of California, Berkeley.

To Dr. Benjamin Carroll, my husband and chief critic, and to Doris Aller, my mother and principal encourager, I am indeed very grateful.

This project was supported by two one-year grants from the National Endowment for the Arts, for the research, writing, and publication of this book. Additional support was provided by the Carl Austin Rietz Foundation, and by the California Academy of Sciences.

Diane Lee Carroll

# INDEX

Burial practices, 78
  textiles, 61
Byzantine
  Empire, Constantinople, 78
  period, 11, 64, 79, 80

# C

Cappadocia, supplies for Roman army in,
  10
Chnem-hotep, 75
Christian Era, 2
Christianity
  militant, 63
  state religion, 11, 57, 61, 78, 79
Christians
  Coptic, 63, 132
  Egyptian, 76
  Melkite, 63
  Monothelite, 63
  persecution of, 78
Churches and Monasteries
  Antinoöpolis site, 102
  Arian Baptistery, Ravenna, 130
  Bawit, Egypt,
    monastery (textile find site), 130
    monastery wall paintings, 6
  Cappella Sanctorum, Rome, 3
  Coptic Monastery of Epiphanius,
    Thebes, 37, 80
  Ibn Tulun mosque, Cairo, 81
  Monastery of Saint Pachomius, 63, 79
  Orphic temple, floor mosaics, 62
  San Vitale, Ravenna, 6, 86, 92
  Sant'Appollinare Nuovo, Ravenna, 6,
    95
  Temple of
    Amon, Siwa Oasis, 79
    Isis, Philae, 79
    Janus, Rome, 76
    Serapis, Canopus (Alexandria), 79
  White monastery, Panapolis (Akmîm),
    128
Classical antiquity, textiles of, 3
Cloaks, 12, 47
Clothing, decorated, 31
Colored garments, depiction in Greek art,
  22
Constantinople, 79
Coptic
  architecture, 3, 65
  artists, 45
  Christian calendar, 60, 77
  Christians, 80
    persecution of, 80, 81, 158, 172, 176
  Church, 63
  definition of, 2
  Egyptians, persecution of, 81, 114
  language of ritual, 81
  period, 30, 36, 170
  sculpture, 3
  socks, 48
  weavers, 81
Coptic textile
  designers, 64

designs, 63, 136
  Greek themes, 57
motifs, see Motifs, Coptic textile
ornamentation, Greek mythological, 65
ornaments, 32
  pagan themes, 62
style, 55
technology, see Textile technology,
  Coptic
Coptic textile corpus
  Christian themes, 57
  size, 2
  source of historical information, 4
  subject matter, 56
  woven textile busts, 6
Coptic textile decoration
  Christian, 57
  from classical antiquity, 65
  themes, mythological, 56
Coptic textile design
  dualism principle, 58
  elements
    acroterion, 124
    aediculae, 120, 123
    amphora motif, 154, 178 (see also
      Motifs, Coptic Textile, vase)
    anchor motif, 176
    animal, fish, and bird motifs, 99, 100,
      102, 104, 106, 110-112, 114, 118,
      120, 124, 128, 130, 132, 134, 148,
      149, 154, 156, 158, 160, 162, 166,
      168, 170, 172, 180
    arcade, 102, 104, 112, 116, 120, 152,
      158, 166
    border, 82, 88, 90, 98, 100, 102, 108,
      111, 112, 114, 118, 124, 132, 134,
      147, 148, 154, 160, 162, 164, 166,
      168, 170, 172, 178, 180
    busts, 120, 124, 168
    cable pattern, 82, 154, 182
    cartouches, 96, 120, 128, 152, 156, 168
    clavus (pl. clavi), 31, 40, 41, 53, 86,
      87, 100, 101, 106, 107, 108, 114,
      120, 124, 136, 137, 150, 152, 156,
      162, 164, 168, 169, 172, (illus) 87,
      121
    cross motif, 102, 104, 108, 176, 180
      Greek, 128, 132, 148, 176
      hooked, 86, 176
      jeweled, 80, 130, 160
    figure motifs, 99
    figures, fabulous, 147 (see also
      Motifs, Coptic textile,
      mythical figures)
    geometric patterns, 92, 94, 120, 128,
      130, 154, 182
    Hetoimasia, 130
    human figures, 102, 108, 110, 112,
      116, 120, 124, 132, 136, 152, 160,
      162, 164, 166, 168
    insects, 160, 166, 168
    interlace patterns, 56, 86, 90, 96, 98,
      180
    jeweled throne motif, 130

jewels motif, 149
knot motifs, 86, 92, 98, 102
Kufic letters, 172
leaf motifs, 62, 182
leaves, 82, 92, 99, 108, 152, 168, 182
lozenges, 86, 100, 106, 120, 128, 152,
  154, 172, 182
meander, 84, 158, 170
Persian motifs, 80
plant motif, 99, 116, 130, 136, 147,
  148, 158, 168
quatrefoil motif, 166, 168, 172, 182
rinceau, 92, 98, 99, 100, 110, 116, 118,
  120
rosettes, 84, 86, 88, 90, 102, 132, 168,
  170, 176
spiral-wave motif, 86, 88, 104, 106,
  108, 114, 124, 128, 150, 156, 162,
  164, 168, 176, 178
stair-step jewel inlay, 134, 136
star, eight-pointed, 86, 92
star, six-pointed, 172
tau motif, 170
trefoils, 86, 120, 147, 168
wreath, 86, 168, 180
(see also Motifs)
Roman contribution, 51
Coptic textiles, 23, 27, 29, 30, 45, 50, 63
  change to Arabic design, 65
  decorative woven items, 58
  designs, monochrome
    figurative, 116
    non-representational, 116
  dubious provenance, 3, 4
  embroidered ornaments, 32
  extant, 13, 52, 57, 79, 180
    chemical analysis, 33
    embellishments, 32
    sources, 50
  historical aspects, 3, 5
  history, 61
  tapestry decoration, 57
  yellow by decree, 81
Coptic tunics, 39, 53, 54, 55 (see also Tunics)
  design schemes, (illus) 40
  evil eye defense devices as decoration,
    55
  extant, 31
  ornament positioning, 54
  ornamentation, 54
Copts, 79
Council of
  Chalcedon, 79
    Fourth Ecumenical, 12, 63, 79
  Constantinople, 79
  Nicaea, 78
Counter-shed, 16, 34, 35, 106
Crapaud, see Ornaments, textile
Crusades, 13, 65, 81
Curtain, 130, 172, 173
  or mantle segment, (color plate) 69
Cushion ornament, 116, 120